OUR INDIVIDUAL FASHION SENSE IS TAILORED TO FIT OUR PERSONALITIES, OUR PERSPECTIVES, OUR PRIORITIES …

HANDSOME HANDBAGS & CREATIVE CARRY-ALLS

… AND OUR PURSES SHOULDN'T BE ANY DIFFERENT. That's why we've compiled a variety of unique handbags that combine the latest colors, styles, and textures to create fresh, innovative looks you won't find anywhere else. Build on these ideas by choosing personalized color and fabric combinations — try classic choices for the office or mix stripes and prints for a free-spirited trip around town. You can even incorporate designer tricks such as reversible fabric for easy coordination or decorative flourishes like trims, fringe, buttons, and charms. And it's all easier than you might think, thanks to the clear instructions that have made Leisure Arts famous in the do-it-yourself industry. So choose your materials, and get ready to create the purse of your dreams!

LEISURE ARTS, INC.
Little Rock, Arkansas

SOPHISTICATED

JUST THE THING FOR A WEEKEND GETAWAY
or a business engagement, this sophisticated travel set
includes a garment bag, a cosmetic bag, and a spacious
carry-all. The classic color scheme suggests style and
poise, while the diamond swirl pattern adds a hint of fun.

SOPHISTICATED GARMENT BAG

1⅝ yds (150 cm) 54"w fabric for outer oval and back (or 2 yds if fabric is directional)

⅝ yd (58 cm) 54"w fabric for inner oval

½ yd (46 cm) 45"w clear vinyl

1⅛ yds (104 cm) 54"w fabric for binding and trim

⅛ yd (12 cm) 45"w craft fleece or 21"w buckram for handle inserts (optional)

100" two-way separating zipper

Tracing paper

⅝" and 1" bias tape makers

Removable fabric marker

Masking tape

Tissue paper

½"w fusible web tape (optional)

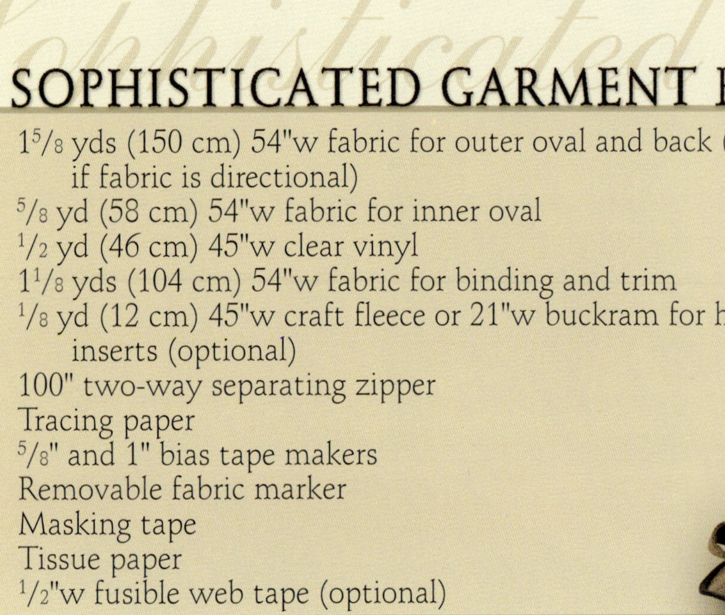

When sewing, match right sides and raw edges and use a ¼" seam allowance unless otherwise indicated. To prevent clear vinyl from sticking to sewing machine, place tissue paper on it; gently tear tissue paper off when finished. We used contrasting thread and materials in our photos for clarity.

1. Cut fabrics as indicated on Cutting Layouts, page 37. Use fabric marker to label wrong side of fabric pieces with letters shown. Label vinyl pieces with masking tape.

2. Using outer curve pattern on page 38, trace solid line and arrows of top portion onto tracing paper. Line arrows up with remaining bottom portion and trace remaining part of line. Stack pieces **B** and **H**. Cut curve as shown.

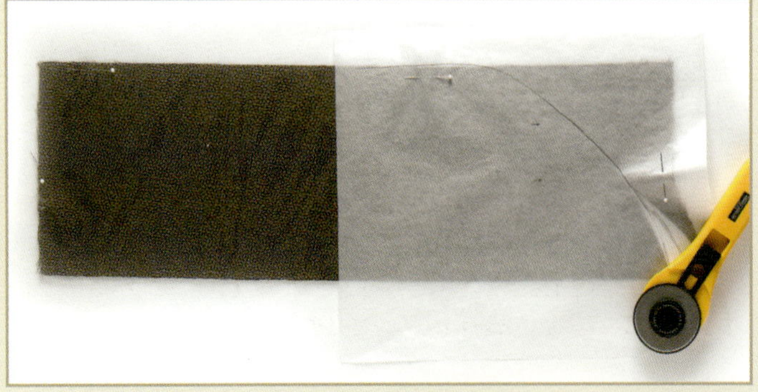

Turn curve pattern over and cut other side. Repeat to cut curve on **E**, then **I**.

3. Trace inner curve pattern, page 38; repeat Step 2 to cut inner curve on one long side of piece **F**.

4. For inside hanger support piece, serge or zigzag stitch vinyl liner **H** to **B** along straight edge. Baste along curved edge.

5. Cut a 1¼"w strip across the diagonal of piece **J**. Use ⅝" bias tape maker to make bias tape from strip.

6. Center **F** on **E**, aligning straight edges; baste **F** to **E**. Place bias tape made from **J** on top of basted curve; topstitch close to each edge.

Cut bias tape flush with raw edges.

7. Stack **F/E** on **I**. Baste ⅛" from all edges.

8. For garment bag bottom, repeat Step 2 to cut outer curve on one short side of **C** and inner curve on one short side of **G**.

9. Center **G** on **C**, aligning straight edges. Cut around **G** to make **C** into a "U" shape. Discard center of **C**.

10. Follow "Making Bias Binding," page 53, to make two 95" lengths of $1^5/_8$"w bias binding from piece **L**.

11. Follow "Attaching Binding," page 54, to attach bias binding to sides and bottom curve of **G**. Attach remaining bias binding to inner curve of **C**.

12. Place right side of zipper against back of bound edge of **G**, aligning edges so that zipper teeth are just outside binding. (Zipper may be longer than needed.) Topstitch through zipper and bias binding.

Repeat to sew remaining side of zipper to **C**. Clip zipper tape around curves.

13. Move zipper pulls to center and trim zipper ends even with fabric edges.

14. Overlapping $1/2$" at the straight edge, baste **F/E/I** garment bag top to **C/G** garment bag bottom. Trim sides even if necessary.

15. Use 1" bias tape maker to make bias tape from strip **M**. Lay strip across seam between garment bag top and garment bag bottom; topstitch close to both long edges of strip to complete garment bag front. Trim ends even with garment bag sides.

16. Stack garment bag front on **A**, wrong sides together. Trim corners of **A** to match garment bag front.

17. Follow "Making Bias Binding," page 53, to make one 146" length of $1^5/_8$"w bias binding from piece **K**.

18. Cut two 5" lengths of binding. Aligning curves, place **B/H** on **A**, with wrong sides of fabrics facing. Attach one length of binding to center of top edge. Attach remaining length of binding to center top edge of garment bag front.

19. Place **A/B/H** and garment bag front together with right sides facing out. Press one short end of remaining binding $1/4$" to wrong side. Beginning with pressed end and overlapping the 5" binding piece by $1/2$", pin binding around the outside raw edges of the garment bag. Trim binding to $3/4$" overlap on remaining side of 5" binding and turn end under $1/4$". Attach binding.

20. Read "Making and Attaching Handles," page 55, to make handles from **D** pieces and sew them in place at top and bottom of garment bag.

SOPHISTICATED CARRY-ALL

$^5/_8$ yd (58 cm) 54"w fabric for lower half of tote and
    handles
$^1/_3$ yd (31 cm) 54"w fabric for upper half of tote
$1^1/_8$ yds (104 cm) 54"w fabric for lining
$^3/_8$ yd (35 cm) 54"w fabric for trim and binding
$^3/_8$ yd (35 cm) 45"w craft fleece
$^2/_3$ yd (62 cm) 21"w buckram or $^1/_8$ yd 45"w craft
   fleece for handle inserts (optional)
26" zipper
$8^1/_4$" x $14^1/_4$" x $^1/_4$" piece of plywood
Removable fabric marker
Fabric glue
$^1/_2$"w fusible web tape (optional)

*When sewing, match right sides and raw edges and use a
$^1/_4$" seam allowance unless otherwise indicated. We used
contrasting thread and materials in our photos for clarity.*

1. Cut fabrics as indicated on Cutting Layouts,
    page 39. Use fabric marker to label wrong side of
    fabric pieces with letters shown.

2. To make one tote side, stack piece **B** (right side
    up) on piece **I** (right side down). Baste $^1/_8$" from
    each edge. Repeat to make remaining tote side
    with **C** and **J**.

3. To make boxing strip, stack piece **A** (right side
    up) on piece **H** (right side down); baste $^1/_8$" from
    each edge.

4. Follow "Sewing Box Corners," page 55, to sew
    tote sides to boxing strip, placing lining
    fabrics together.

5. To make binding, sew short ends of **N** pieces
    together to form one continuous length. Press
    seam allowances open.

6. Cut two $9^1/_2$" and four 10" lengths of binding.
    Follow "Attaching Binding," page 54, to attach
    $9^1/_2$" lengths to bottom edges of tote. Follow
    "Overlapping Binding," page 54, to attach one
    10" length of binding to each remaining raw
    edge.

7. To make upper half of tote, stack and pin piece **F**
    (right side up) on piece **K** (right side down).
    Repeat to stack **G** on **L**. Serge or zigzag stitch
    each short edge. Using a $^1/_2$" seam allowance
    with lining fabrics facing out, sew **F/K** to **G/L**
    along each short end to form tube. Press seam
    allowances open; topstitch $^3/_8$" from seam on
    each side. Turn tube right side out.

8. To attach trim to bottom edge of upper tote,
    press one long side of **S** $^1/_2$" to wrong side. Press
    one short end of **S** $^1/_4$" to wrong side. Beginning
    with pressed end and using a $^1/_2$" seam
    allowance, sew long raw edge of **S** to one long
    edge of upper tote.

9. To bind top edge of upper tote, cut a 51" length
    of binding. Press one short end of binding $^1/_4$" to
    wrong side. Beginning with pressed end, attach
    binding to remaining long edge of upper tote.

10. Serge or zigzag stitch all sides of **O** and **P**. Fold each short end $^1/_2$" to wrong side; press.

11. To make zipper placket pieces, press one long raw edge of pieces **O** and **P** $^1/_2$" to wrong side. Centering length of zipper, place folded edge of **O** against side of zipper. Using zipper foot, sew **O** to zipper $^3/_8$" from fold.

Repeat to sew **P** to remaining side of zipper.

12. Press each side of pieces **Q** and **R** $^1/_4$" to wrong side. Fold square around ends of zipper; topstitch in place.

13. Center zipper placket inside bound edge of upper tote. Pin along length so that zipper teeth extend $^1/_4$" above bound edge. Topstitch along binding stitching.

Unzip zipper and repeat to attach remaining side of placket to remaining upper tote side.

14. Read "Making and Attaching Handles," page 55, to make handles from **D** and **E** pieces and attach to top of upper tote. Sew an "X" through squares at the base of each handle.

15. With lining fabrics together, sew unbound edge of upper tote to tote bottom (A/B/C).

16. Press trim **S** over seam; whipstitch in place.

17. For bottom stabilizer, wrap **T** around plywood, folding and pleating corners; glue in place. Repeat with **M**. Insert covered plywood into bottom of tote.

SOPHISTICATED COSMETIC BAG

$^1/_3$ yd (31 cm) 54"w fabric for decorative top
$^7/_8$ yd (80 cm) 54"w fabric for front and back
$1^1/_4$ yds (115 cm) 45"w clear vinyl
$^3/_8$ yd (35 cm) 54"w fabric for binding
$1^1/_8$ yds (104 cm) of $^1/_2$"w hem tape
$1^1/_3$ yds (123 cm) of 1"w hook and loop fastener tape
Three 14" zippers
Wooden hanger, cut down to 13"
Removable fabric marker
Masking tape
Tissue paper

When sewing, match right sides and raw edges and use a $^1/_4$" seam allowance unless otherwise indicated. To prevent clear vinyl from sticking to sewing machine, place tissue paper on it; gently tear tissue paper off when finished. We used contrasting thread and materials in our photos for clarity.

1. Cut fabrics as indicated on Cutting Layouts, page 40. Use fabric marker to label wrong side of fabric pieces with letters shown. Label vinyl pieces with masking tape.

2. To make binding, sew short ends of **N** pieces together to form one continuous length. Press seam allowances open.

3. With wrong sides together and angled ends aligned, stack **B** on **C**. Baste $^1/_8$" from each edge.

4. For removable pocket, cut two $13^1/_2$" lengths of binding. Follow "Attaching Binding," page 54, to attach binding to one long edge of **D** and **G**. Place front side of one zipper against back of **D**, aligning edges so that zipper teeth are just above folded edge of binding.

Use zipper foot to sew along binding close to zipper. Repeat to attach remaining edge of zipper to bound edge of **G**. Move zipper pull to center and trim zipper ends even with vinyl.

5. Cut a 12$^{1}/_{2}$" length of hook and loop fastener. Cut loop side to 10$^{1}/_{4}$"; set hook length aside. Place loop side of fastener face up and centered next to binding on **G**. Topstitch down each long side of tape.

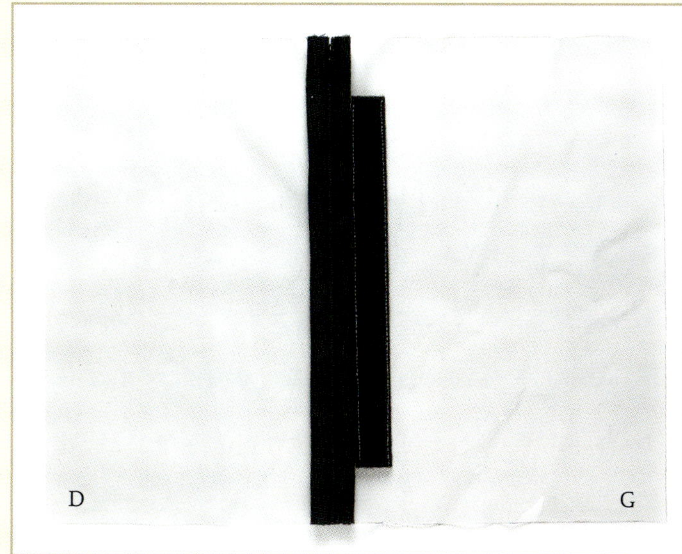

6. Fold **D** and **G** so cut long edges are aligned and zipper is on the outside of the fold. Cut a 13$^{1}/_{2}$" length of binding; attach binding to long cut edges.

7. Cut a 9" length of binding; fold long raw edges to meet in middle. Fold in half lengthwise; press. Topstitch very close to each long edge. Fold in half widthwise to form loop. Sew ends of loop in place at top end of zipper on **D/G**.

8. Cut two 9" lengths of binding. Fold short ends of each length $^{1}/_{4}$" to wrong side. Attach binding to each short edge of **D/G**. Removable pocket **D/G** will attach to **B** with the hook and loop fastener strips. Set removable pocket aside.

9. For attached pockets, repeat Step 4 with **E/H** and **F/I**. Repeat Step 6 on **F/I** only.

10. For pleated pocket, cut one 31$^{1}/_{2}$" length of binding. Attach binding to one long edge of piece **L** for top of pocket.

11. Cut two 9" lengths of hem tape. Sew one length of tape 10$^{5}/_{8}$" from each short end of **L**.

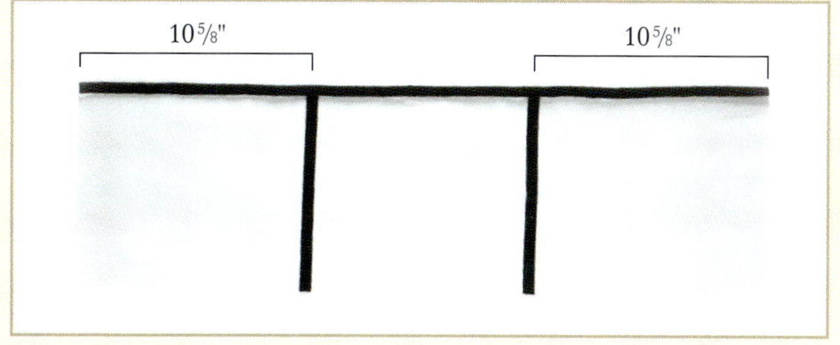

12. Mark pleats with pins at measurements shown.

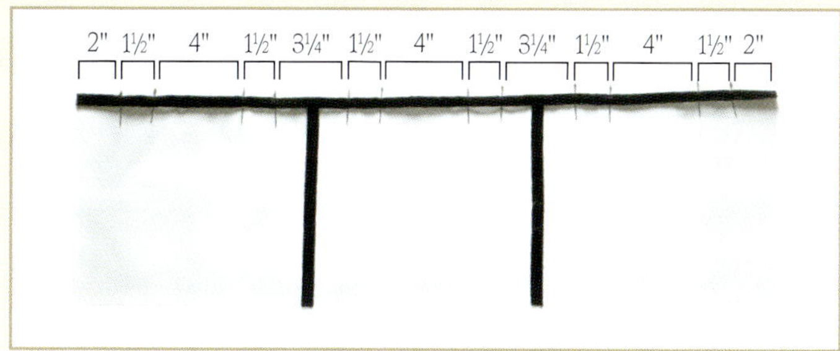

Fold pleats as shown in photo, page 8. Lay **L** across width of **B/C**; adjust pleats as necessary to fit width exactly. Remove from **B/C**.

13. Cut one 13$^{1}/_{2}$" length of binding; attach binding to bottom pleated edge of **L**.

14. Repeat Steps 10–13 to make another pleated pocket from piece **M**.

15. Fold pocket **E/H** so long cut edges are aligned and zipper is on outside of fold. Align pocket **E/H** along bottom straight edge on "B" side of **B/C**. Baste pocket **E/H** to **B/C** ⅛" from edge on each side.

16. Cut a 13½" length of binding; attach to bottom edges of **B/C** and **E/H**. Cut a 6" length of hook and loop fastener. Discard loop side; pin hook side along center bottom of **C**; topstitch in place along binding stitching.

17. Measure 9¾" from bottom on "B" side of **B/C**; center hook side of fastener from Step 5 across width. Topstitch each long side of tape.

18. Pin pleated pocket **L** to **B/C** right above the sewn hook tape. Baste each side in place ⅛" from edge. Topstitch along hem tape to anchor pockets. Topstitch ⅛" from folded edge of bottom binding.

19. Place **F/I** 2½" above top edge of pleated pocket **L** with zipper at top. Baste each side in place ⅛" from edge. Topstitch along both edges of bottom binding.

20. Repeat Step 18 to sew pleated pocket **M** to **B/C** 2½" above pocket **F/I**.

21. Cut a 3" length of hook and loop fastener. Aligning angled ends, place liner **J** on "B" side of **B/C**; baste along side and top edges. Center hook side of fastener on bottom edge of liner **J**; topstitch fastener along all edges. Cut a 3" length of binding; attach to top edge of **B/C/J**. Cut ends of binding even with angled sides of fabric.

22. Cut a 13½" length of binding. Place liner **K** on wrong side of **A**. Attach binding to long straight edges. Cut a 3" length of binding. Attach binding to short straight edges. Cut ends of binding even with angled sides of fabric. This will be the top. Center and topstitch loop side of fastener from Step 21 to bottom edge of liner on **A/K**, making sure hook and loop pieces align when **A/K** is placed on **B/C/J**.

23. Cut two 3" lengths of hook and loop fastener; discard loop sides. Working on "C" side of **B/C**, measure 3½" down and 1¼" in from each lower side of angled end. Topstitch hook side of fasteners as shown.

24. Turn organizer over to work on "B" side again. Stack A/K on B/C/J with **K** and **J** facing. Cut two $6^1/2$" lengths of binding. Press short ends $^1/4$" to wrong side. Attach binding to each top angled edge.

25. Cut two 50" lengths of binding. Press short ends $^1/4$" to wrong side. Attach binding to each side edge of cosmetic bag.

26. Cut two $8^1/2$" lengths of hook and loop fastener. Discard hook side. Working on "C" side of cosmetic bag, topstitch each loop side of fastener tape at bottom of **C** as shown.

UNTAMED

GIVE THE WORLD A GLIMPSE OF YOUR WILD SIDE with a decidedly untamed purse. Eschewing subtlety, this daring purse thrives on a crazy combination of colors, patterns, and textures, including a lush suede fringe.

UNTAMED

$^1\!/_3$ yd (31 cm) 54"w fabric for purse front
$^1\!/_3$ yd (31 cm) 54"w fabric for boxing strip and handles
$^1\!/_4$ yd (23 cm) 54"w fabric for binding and trim
$^1\!/_3$ yd (31 cm) 54"w fabric for purse back and pocket
$^1\!/_2$ yd (46 cm) 54"w fabric for lining
$^1\!/_4$ yd (23 cm) 54"w fabric for cuff
$^1\!/_4$ yd (23 cm) 45"w batting
$^2\!/_3$ yd (62 cm) 21"w buckram or $^1\!/_8$ yd (12 cm) 45"w
    craft fleece for handle inserts (optional)
$^7\!/_8$ yd (80 cm) of $2^1\!/_2$"w suede loop fringe
$2^3\!/_4$" x $9^3\!/_4$" x $^1\!/_{16}$" foam board
Magnetic snap kit
Six $^5\!/_8$" dia. buttons
Removable fabric marker
Fabric glue
$^1\!/_2$"w fusible web tape (optional)

When sewing, match right sides and raw edges and use a $^1\!/_4$" seam allowance unless otherwise indicated. We used contrasting thread in our photos for clarity.

1. Cut fabrics as indicated on Cutting Layouts, page 41. Use fabric marker to label wrong side of fabric pieces with letters shown.

2. To make binding, sew short ends of **E** pieces together to form one continuous length. Press seam allowances open.

3. For pocket, cut two 6" and two $5^1\!/_2$" lengths of binding. Follow "Attaching Binding," page 54, to attach one 6" length of binding to each long raw edge of pocket **H**. Follow "Overlapping Binding," page 54, to attach one $5^1\!/_2$" length of binding to each short edge of pocket **H**. With right sides facing up, center pocket on lining **I**; topstitch pocket in place along sides and bottom.

4. To make purse front, stack piece **A** (right side up) on piece **J** (right side down). Baste $^1\!/_8$" from each edge. Repeat to make purse back from **G** and **I**.

5. To make boxing strip, stack piece **B** (right side up) on piece **K** (right side down). Baste $^1\!/_8$" from each edge.

6. Follow "Sewing Box Corners," page 55, to sew purse front and purse back to boxing strip, placing lining fabrics together.

7. Serge or zigzag stitch remaining raw edges of sewn purse.

8. Cut two $10^1\!/_2$" lengths of binding. Attach binding to each long seam allowance on bottom of purse. Cut four $8^1\!/_2$" lengths of binding. Press ends of each length $^1\!/_4$" to wrong side. Attach binding to side seam allowances.

9. Stack piece **M** (right side up) on piece **O**; serge or zigzag stitch all edges together. Repeat with **N** and **P**.

10. Stack **M/O** on **N/P** with right sides of cuff fabric together. Sew the angled sides together to make cuff.

Press fabric seam allowances open and turn right side out.

11. Trimming length as needed and gently easing fringe around corners, sew fringe to long edge of cuff so that only $1/4$" of bound fringe edge overlaps cuff. Trim bound edge of fringe even with cuff.

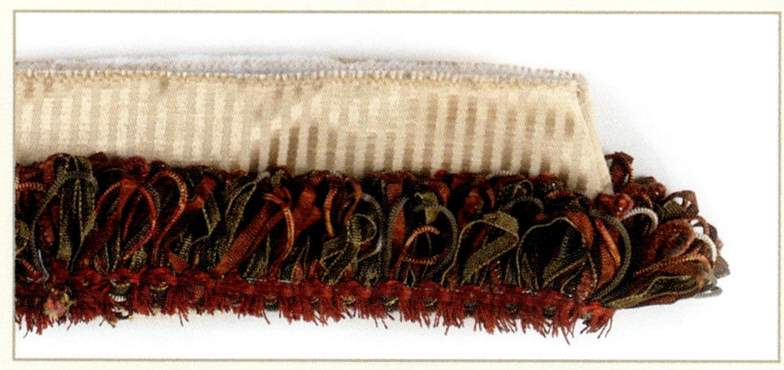

12. With right side of cuff facing the lining of the purse, place cuff inside purse. Line up seams of cuff with sides of purse. Using a $1/2$" seam allowance, sew cuff to purse.

Flip cuff over seam to outside of purse.

13. Follow Step 2 of "Making and Attaching Handles," page 55, to make handles from **C** and **D**.

14. Press all edges of each **F** piece $1/4$" to wrong side. Press each piece in half widthwise.

15. Pin one **F** piece over one end of handle; pin another **F** piece over other end of handle. Pin handle inside purse where desired.

Topstitch handle in place, stitching through lining and purse and being careful not to catch cuff in stitching. Repeat with remaining **F** pieces and remaining handle.

16. Sew three buttons to cuff front and back. Attach magnetic snap to lining and purse beneath cuff.

17. For bottom stabilizer, wrap **L** around foam board, folding and pleating corners; glue in place. Insert covered foam board into bottom of purse.

SLEEK

THOUGH IT'S MADE OF UPHOLSTERY FABRIC, THIS SILVERY HANDBAG STILL MANAGES A SLEEK, ELEGANT LOOK, thanks to a subtle monochromatic color scheme. Matching fringe adds a distinctive flourish, and coordinating buttons draw attention to the pocketbook's noteworthy shape.

SLEEK

$^3/_4$ yd (69 cm) 54"w rubberized fabric for purse
    body, pocket, and handle
$^5/_8$ yd (58 cm) 54"w rubberized fabric for cuff
    and fringe
1 yd (92 cm) 21"w buckram
$^5/_8$ yd (58 cm) 54"w fabric for binding and lining
$^1/_2$ yd (46 cm) 45"w craft fleece
14" zipper
Six 1" dia. buttons
$2^3/_4$" x $5^3/_4$" x $^1/_{16}$" foam board
Removable fabric marker
Fabric glue
Tracing paper
$^1/_2$"w fusible web tape (optional)

*When sewing, match right sides and raw edges and use a
$^1/_4$" seam allowance unless otherwise indicated. We used
contrasting thread and materials in our photos for clarity.*

1. Cut fabrics as indicated on Cutting Layouts, page 42. Use fabric marker to label wrong side of fabric pieces with letters shown.

2. To make binding, sew short ends of **T** pieces together to form one continuous length. Press seam allowances open.

3. For pocket, cut four $5^1/_2$" lengths of binding. Follow "Attaching Binding," page 54, to attach one $5^1/_2$" length of binding to each long raw edge of pocket **D**. Follow "Overlapping Binding," page 54, to attach one remaining length to each short edge of pocket **D**. With right sides facing up, center pocket on lining **N**; topstitch pocket in place along sides and bottom.

4. To make purse front, stack piece **A** (right side down), piece **K**, then piece **N** (right side up). Baste $^1/_8$" from each edge. Repeat to make purse back from pieces **B**, **L**, and **O**.

5. To make boxing strip, stack piece **E** (right side down), piece **M**, then piece **S** (right side up); baste $^1/_8$" from each edge.

6. Follow "Sewing Box Corners," page 55, to sew purse front and purse back to boxing strip, placing lining fabrics together.

7. Cut two $6^1/_2$" lengths of binding. Attach binding to bottom seam allowances of sewn purse. Cut four 13" lengths of binding. Press ends of each length $^1/_4$" to wrong side. Attach binding to side seam allowances.

8. Use fabric marker to mark a line 2" from top of purse on lining.

9. To make cuff, trace large triangular piece, page 43, onto tracing paper, including arrows. Line up arrows with remaining pattern piece; trace remaining lines. Use tracing paper pattern to cut cuff pieces from **G**, **H**, **U**, and **V**. Stack **U** on wrong side of **G** and **V** on wrong side of **H**; baste $^1/_8$" from each edge.

10. Matching fabric sides of **G/U** and **H/V** pieces, sew the angled sides together to complete cuff.

Turn right side out. Serge or zigzag stitch top straight edge of cuff.

11. To make bias trim, cut three $1^1/_2$"w strips along the $45°$ diagonal of piece **C**. Sew short ends together to make one continuous bias strip. With wrong sides together, pin strip in half lengthwise.

12. Pin bias strip along bottom edge of cuff, allowing extra fullness for the points.

13. Pin fringe piece **J** over bias strip and cuff. Using a $1/_2$" seam allowance, sew **J** and bias strip to cuff.

14. Place right side of cuff next to purse lining inside purse with seams centered on sides. Align straight edge of cuff with line drawn on lining in Step 8. Sewing through all layers, sew cuff to purse; flip cuff to outside of purse.

15. To make zipper placket pieces, fold piece **P** in half lengthwise with right sides together. Sew along each short end.

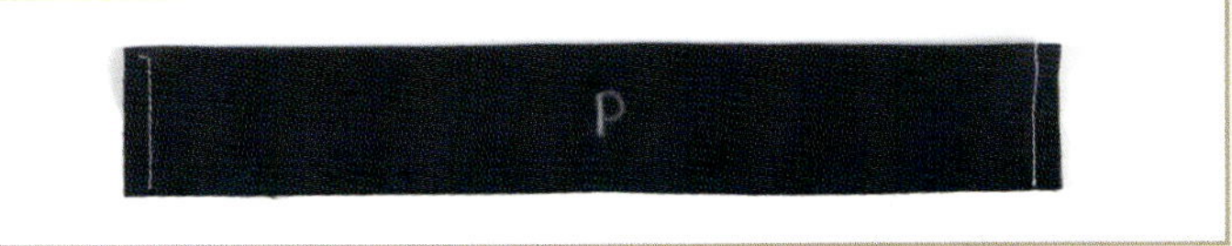

Turn inside out. Serge or zigzag stitch unfinished long edges together. Repeat with piece **Q**.

16. Centering the length, lay folded edge of one placket piece next to teeth on zipper; topstitch.

Repeat with remaining placket piece on remaining side of zipper.

17. Press each side of **R** pieces $1/_4$" to wrong side. Fold square around ends of zipper to hold sides together; topstitch.

18. Center zipper placket in purse. Align one serged edge of placket with seam of cuff; sew in place.

Open zipper and repeat to sew remaining side of placket on opposite side of purse.

19. Follow "Making and Attaching Handles," page 55, to sew handle from piece **F** and attach one end of handle to each side of purse. Do not use handle inserts on this purse; the layers will be too thick to sew through.

20. Sew three buttons to each pointed end of cuff.

21. Cut fringe. We followed the grooved pattern on our fabric to cut fringe; you can also measure to cut $1/_4$"w fringe.

22. For bottom stabilizer, wrap piece **I** around foam board, folding and pleating corners; glue in place. Insert covered foam board into bottom of purse.

CHIC

AN ECLECTIC MIXTURE OF FASHION'S HOTTEST COLORS AND FABRICS, this ultra-chic pocketbook is sure to be the envy of all your friends. Soft looped fringe, smooth bamboo handles, and a faux suede body are surprisingly complementary and supremely touchable.

CHIC

3/8 yd (35 cm) 54"w faux suede for purse body
1/3 yd (31 cm) 54"w fabric for binding and trim
1/2 yd (46 cm) 54"w fabric for lining and pocket
1/3 yd (31 cm) 54"w fabric for trim and handles
1/2 yd (46 cm) 21"w buckram
7/8 yd (80 cm) of 2"w loop fringe
Six 7/8" dia. shank-style buttons
Two 12 1/2" bamboo handles
2 3/4" x 16 1/4" x 1/16" foam board
Removable fabric marker
Hot glue gun
Fabric glue
1/2"w fusible web tape (optional)

When sewing, match right sides and raw edges and use a 1/4" seam allowance unless otherwise indicated.

1. Cut fabrics as indicated on Cutting Layouts, page 44. Use fabric marker to label wrong side of fabric pieces with letters shown.

2. To make binding, sew short ends of **E** pieces together to form one continuous length. Press seam allowances open.

3. For inside pocket, cut two 7" lengths and two 5 1/2" lengths of binding. Follow "Attaching Binding," page 54, to attach 7" lengths of binding to each long raw edge of pocket **G**. Follow "Overlapping Binding," page 54, to attach one 5 1/2" length to each short edge of pocket **G**. With right sides facing up, center pocket on one **F** piece; topstitch pocket in place along sides and bottom.

4. To make purse front, stack one piece **A** (right side down), one piece **L**, then one piece **F** (right side up). Baste 1/8" from each edge. Repeat to make purse back.

5. To make boxing strip, stack piece **C** (right side down), then piece **I** (right side up); baste 1/8" from each edge.

6. Follow "Sewing Box Corners," page 55, to sew purse front and purse back to boxing strip, placing lining fabrics together.

7. Cut two 17" lengths of binding. Attach binding to long seam allowances of purse bottom. Cut four 7" lengths of binding. Press short ends of each length 1/4" to wrong side. Attach binding to side seam allowances.

8. To assemble purse trim piece, cut a 6 1/2" length and a 6 3/4" length of binding. Attach 6 1/2" length binding to one short edge of one **K** trim piece. Press one short end of 6 3/4" length 1/4" to wrong side. With pressed end overlapping bound edge, attach this length of binding to remaining short edge of **K** trim piece.

9. Cut a 15" length of fringe. Pin fringe (right side up) to back short edges of trim piece; topstitch to trim piece, stitching over previous stitching. Cut off any excess fringe. Sew a button to corner of trim piece. Center and baste trim piece to purse front.

10. Repeat Steps 8 and 9 to assemble and attach remaining trim piece to purse back.

11. Cut one 41" length of binding. Press one end $1/4$" to wrong side. Beginning with pressed end, attach binding to top edge of purse. Trim excess binding as needed.

12. Follow Step 2 of "Making and Attaching Handles," page 55, to make handles from **J** pieces. Do not use handle inserts on this purse; the layers will be too thick to sew through.

13. To make handle extensions, sew one **D** to one **B** along one short side and two long sides. Turn right side out; press raw edges $1/4$" to the wrong side. Trimming as needed, insert one **M** piece into sewn **D/B**. Repeat for a total of four.

14. Fold each extension in half widthwise; mark center with a pin and unfold. With suede towards purse lining and open end up, line up pin with top bound edge of purse; topstitch along center of extension.

15. Insert each end of one handle **J** $1/2$" into center of open end of extensions on front of purse. Refold extension pieces; topstitch across top edge, catching handle **J** in seam. Repeat with remaining handle **J** and extensions.

16. Sew one button to inner corner of each extension.

17. Hot glue bamboo handles into extension pieces.

18. For bottom stabilizer, wrap **H** around foam board, folding and pleating corners; use fabric glue to adhere in place. Insert covered foam board into bottom of purse.

THEATRICAL

LIGHT-HEARTED BY NATURE, this theatrical purse assures the world that you don't take life too seriously. The textured cuff, reminiscent of a jester's cap, contributes a sense of drama, while assorted charms add an air of pure whimsy.

THEATRICAL

1/2 yd (46 cm) 54"w faux suede for purse
   body and handle
1/2 yd (46 cm) 54"w fabric for cuff
1/3 yd (31 cm) 54"w fabric for lining
1/2 yd (46 cm) 45"w craft fleece
8 assorted charms or buttons
3³/₄" x 2¹/₄" x ¹/₄" foam board
Removable fabric marker
Tracing paper
¹/₂"w fusible web tape (optional)

When sewing, match right sides and raw edges and use a ¹/₂" seam allowance unless otherwise indicated. We used contrasting thread in our photos for clarity.

1. Cut fabrics as indicated on Cutting Layouts, page 45. Use fabric marker to label wrong side of fabric pieces with letters shown.

2. To make purse, align one short edge of boxing strip **C** with top edge of purse front **A**. Pin boxing strip to purse front. At first corner, make a ³/₈" deep clip on boxing strip ¹/₂" from corner. Pivot and stretch boxing strip to turn corner and continue matching raw edges and pinning. Repeat at remaining corner. Sew boxing strip in place. At each corner, shorten stitches to reinforce and stitch diagonally across corner instead of pivoting. Repeat to sew boxing strip **C** to purse back **B**. Topstitch ¹/₁₆" from each seam.

3. To make lining, repeat Step 2 to sew lining front **I** and lining back **J** to boxing strip **K**.

4. To make cuff, trace large part of cuff pattern and arrows, page 46, onto tracing paper. Line up arrows with remaining pattern piece; trace and cut out. Draw around pattern on wrong side of **E** and **F**. Stack piece **E** (right side down) on **G** (right side up). Add **L** and **M** to the bottom of the stack. Stack piece **F** (right side down) on **H** (right side up). Add **N** and **O** to the bottom of the stack. Cut out **only** straight sides of pattern along drawn lines.

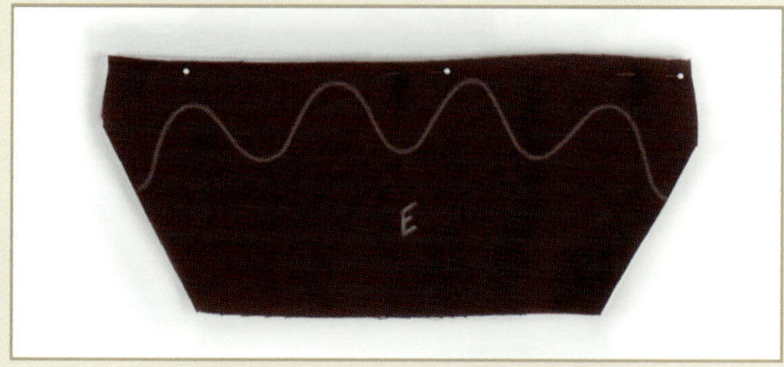

5. Sewing only along short sides, sew **E** to **F** to form a tube. Repeat to sew **G** to **H**, **L** to **M**, and **N** to **O**. Press fabric seam allowances open.

6. Matching side seams, slide **G/H** inside **E/F** with right sides facing. Slide **L/M** and **N/O** inside cuff fabrics. Sew along drawn curved lines, leaving straight edge open. Cut fabric and fleece ¹/₄" outside sewn lines. Clip curves.

Turn right side out.

7. Follow Step 2 of "Making and Attaching Handles," page 55, to make purse handle using **D**. Do not use handle inserts on this purse; the layers will be too thick to sew through. Cut **D** in half lengthwise to make two handles.

8. With lining right side out, slip cuff over lining. Arrange cuff so that seams are centered on each side of boxing strip. Insert ends of handles between cuff and lining at seams.

Sew cuff to lining along straight edge, catching handle ends in stitching. Turn lining wrong side out.

9. For bottom stabilizer, insert foam board in bottom of purse. Matching seams, slide lining into purse; sew in place ¹/₂" from top raw edge of purse.

10. Fold cuff over purse. Hand sew a charm or button to each point of cuff.

EXOTIC

THE KEY TO THIS PURSE'S EXOTIC STYLING is all in the trim. Lush bullion fringe highlights the details of the contrasting fabrics, and natural wooden beads echo the Moroccan theme established by the exquisite decorative flap.

EXOTIC

¹/₄ yd (23 cm) 54"w fabric for decorative flap
¹/₃ yd (31 cm) 54"w fabric for binding and trim
⁵/₈ yd (58 cm) 54"w fabric for purse body and handles
¹/₂ yd (46 cm) 54"w fabric for lining and pocket
¹/₃ yd (31 cm) 45"w clear vinyl for pockets
¹/₄ yd (23 cm) 45"w craft fleece
²/₃ yd (62 cm) 21"w buckram for handle inserts
   (optional)
1¹/₈ yds (104 cm) of 2¹/₂"w bullion fringe
¹/₂ yd (46 cm) beaded fringe
Magnetic snap kit
3¹/₄" x 14³/₄" x ¹/₁₆" foam board
Removable fabric marker
Masking tape
Tissue paper
Tracing paper
Fabric glue
¹/₂"w fusible web tape (optional)

When sewing, match right sides and raw edges and use a ¹/₄" seam allowance unless otherwise indicated. To prevent clear vinyl from sticking to sewing machine, place tissue paper on it; gently tear tissue paper off when finished.

1. Cut fabrics as indicated on Cutting Layouts, page 47. Use fabric marker to label wrong side of fabric pieces with letters shown. Label vinyl pieces with masking tape.

2. To make binding, sew short ends of **I** pieces together to form one continuous length. Press seam allowances open.

3. For lining pocket, cut two 8" and two 5¹/₂" lengths of binding. Follow "Attaching Binding," page 54, to attach 8" lengths of binding to each long raw edge of pocket piece **R**. Follow "Overlapping Binding," page 54, to attach one 5¹/₂" length to each short edge of pocket. With right sides facing up, center pocket on lining **P**; topstitch pocket in place along sides and bottom.

4. For vinyl pockets, cut a 21¹/₂" length of binding. Attach binding to one long edge of pocket piece **T**. Use pins to mark pleats as shown.

Fold pleats as shown. Pin wrong side of pocket **T** on right side of lining **Q**. Topstitch center of pleats between the folds.

5. To make purse front, stack piece **J** (right side up) on piece **P** (right side down). Baste ¹⁄₈" from each edge. Repeat to make purse back from **K** and **Q**.

6. To make boxing strip, stack piece **M** (right side up) on piece **S** (right side down); baste ¹⁄₈" from each edge.

7. Follow "Sewing Box Corners," page 55, to sew purse back and purse front to boxing strip, placing lining fabrics together.

8. Cut two 15¹⁄₂" lengths of binding. Attach binding to bottom seam allowances of sewn purse. Cut four 12¹⁄₂" lengths of binding. Press ends of each length ¹⁄₄" to wrong side. Attach binding to side seam allowances of sewn purse.

9. Beginning and ending at center of back, sew bullion fringe to top of purse so that only ¹⁄₄" of bound edge overlaps top of purse. Trim any excess fringe. If bound edge of bullion fringe is wider than ¹⁄₄", trim to ¹⁄₄".

10. Cut a 39" length of binding. Press one short end ¹⁄₄" to wrong side. Beginning with pressed end of binding at the center back of purse, attach binding to top of purse. Trim any excess binding.

11. Center and attach magnetic snap pieces near the top of the front and back of purse lining.

12. Trace decorative flap pattern, page 48, onto tracing paper. If decorative flap fabric is directional, align pattern with point down as you cut flaps from **A**, **B**, **C**, and **D**. Use pattern to cut pieces **U** and **V**. Baste beaded fringe to bottom edges of pieces **A** and **B** as shown.

13. Stack piece **A** (wrong side up) on piece **C** (wrong side down) and place **U** on top. Leaving top edge open, sew pieces together. Clip corners and turn; serge or zigzag stitch short straight edges together to complete flap. Repeat with **B**, **D**, and **V**.

14. Center top edge of flap on inside front of purse; stitch along short straight edge.

Turn flap to outside of purse. Repeat with remaining flap on inside back of purse.

15. Follow Step 2 of "Making and Attaching Handles," page 55, to make handles from pieces **N** and **O**.

16. Press all edges of **E**, **F**, **G**, and **H** ¹⁄₄" to wrong side. Fold each piece in half widthwise.

17. Pin **E** over one end of handle; pin **F** over other end of handle. Pin handle inside purse where desired. Topstitch handle in place, stitching through all layers and being careful not to catch fringe in stitching. Repeat with **G**, **H**, and remaining handle.

18. For bottom stabilizer, wrap **L** around foam board, folding and pleating corners; glue in place. Insert covered foam board into bottom of purse.

COSMOPOLITAN

OUR COSMOPOLITAN CARRY-ALL IS NOT FOR THE FAINT OF HEART —
the striking animal prints make a bold statement, even in a crowd. Energetic styling and
a roomy interior make this bag an ideal choice for a woman who's always on the go.

COSMOPOLITAN

¹/₃ yd (31 cm) 54"w fabric for upper half of tote
¹/₂ yd (46 cm) 54"w fabric for handle
1¹/₈ yds (104 cm) 54"w fabric for lower half of tote
¹/₄ yd (23 cm) 54"w fabric for binding and trim
¹/₂ yd (46 cm) 45"w craft fleece
1¹/₂ yds (138 cm) of 1¹/₂"w brush fringe
1⁵/₈ yds (150 cm) of 1"w gimp
28" zipper
10" x 14³/₄" x ¹/₄" piece of plywood with rounded corners
Removable fabric marker
Fabric glue

When sewing, match right sides and raw edges and use a ¹/₄" seam allowance unless otherwise indicated. We used contrasting thread and materials in our photos for clarity.

1. Cut fabrics as indicated on Cutting Layouts, page 49. Use fabric marker to label wrong side of fabric pieces with letters shown.

2. For lower half of tote, serge or zigzag stitch one long edge of **E** and **F**. Mark right side of fabric ¹/₄" from corners opposite serged edges; this side will be the bottom. Repeat on **G** and **H**.

3. With wrong sides together and serged edges aligned, sew **G** and **H** to short sides of **E**, stopping at marks.

Repeat to sew **G** and **H** to short sides of **F** to form a tube.

4. With wrong sides together, pin lower half of tote to **I**. Sew lower half of tote to **I** between marks.

5. Cut two 11" lengths and two 15³/₄" lengths of binding from one **K** piece. Beginning and ending ¹/₄" from ends, follow "Attaching Binding," page 54, to attach binding to seam allowances on bottom of tote.

6. Cut four 11¹/₄" lengths of binding from remaining **K** piece. Press one short end of each length ¹/₄" to wrong side. Follow "Overlapping Binding," page 54, to attach binding to side seam allowances with pressed end at bottom.

7. Sew brush fringe to right side of serged edges on lower half of tote so that only ¼" of bound edge overlaps top of purse. Trim bound edge of fringe even with tote.

8. Serge or zigzag stitch all sides of **A**. Sew short ends together to form a tube. Press seam allowances open.

9. With right sides together and seam of **A** centered on tote back, sew **A** to lower half of tote.

10. For zipper placket, serge or zigzag stitch both long raw edges of **L** and **M** pieces.

11. Center and fold **M** pieces lengthwise around raw edges of **A** at each side of bag; topstitch.

12. Press short edges of **L** pieces ¼" to the wrong side. Press one long edge of each **L** piece ¼" to wrong side. Trim top of zipper to ¼" above top stops. Wrapping short end of one **L** piece around raw edge of zipper, pin long folded edge next to teeth on zipper. Use zipper foot to stitch in place.

Repeat with remaining **L** piece on other side of zipper.

13. For loop, press **O** in half lengthwise; open. Press short edges of **O** ¼" to wrong side. Press long edges of **O** to meet in middle; fold in half again and topstitch along folded edges. Mark center of one **M** piece. Sew ends of **O** to either side of mark on inside of purse.

14. Press remaining edges of **L** $^3/_4$" to wrong side. Place one fold over edge of one long side of **A**, with top of zipper $^1/_4$" from edge of loop. Topstitch along long edge $^1/_4$" from fold. Repeat for other **L** piece.

15. For handle, sew short ends of **B**, **C**, and **D** together to form a tube. With wrong sides together, press in half lengthwise; open. Press long raw edges to meet in middle of strip. Fold in half lengthwise; topstitch $^1/_8$" from each long edge to form continuous handle.

16. Press long raw edges of each **N** piece to meet in middle. These pieces will reinforce the gimp in places where the handle is threaded between the gimp and the bag. Measure around top of bag along topstitching. Cut gimp this length plus $^1/_2$". Sew short ends of gimp together. Lay gimp flat with seam at center of back. Mark $6^1/_2$" in from folds of gimp. Sew **N** pieces to back of gimp, wrong sides together, at these marks.

17. Matching seam of gimp with seam of **A**, begin pinning gimp along top edge of bag. The sections that are backed with **N** pieces should be looped up; thread handle through these sections as you reach them and continue pinning.

Sew gimp in place along top and bottom edges, being careful not to catch handle in stitching.

18. Sew one side of handle in place on bag bottom. Lay out tote and pin remaining side of handle to tote bottom. Sew remaining side of handle in place.

19. For bottom stabilizer, wrap **P** around plywood, folding and pleating corners; glue in place. Repeat with **J**. Insert covered plywood into bottom of tote.

SOPHISTICATED GARMENT BAG
(shown on page 4)
cutting layouts

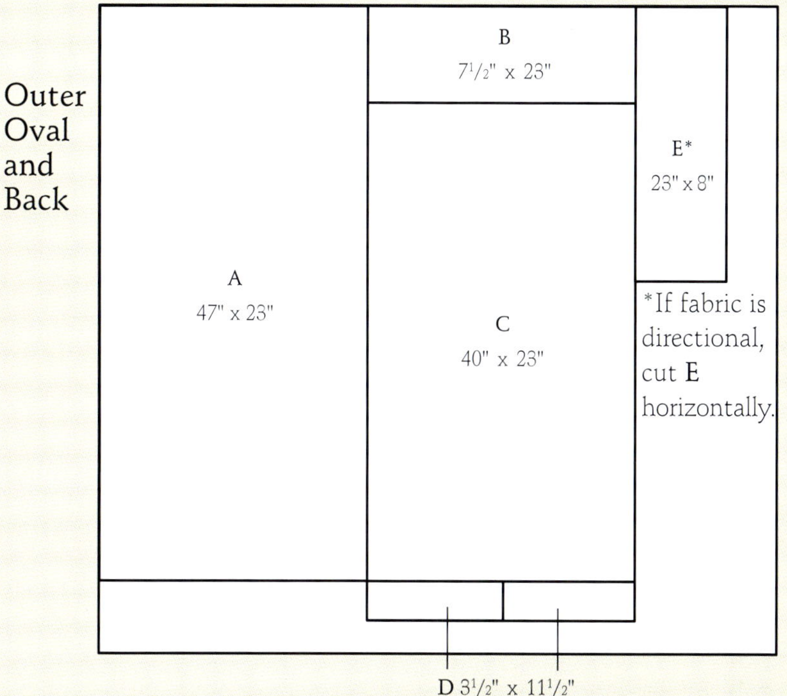

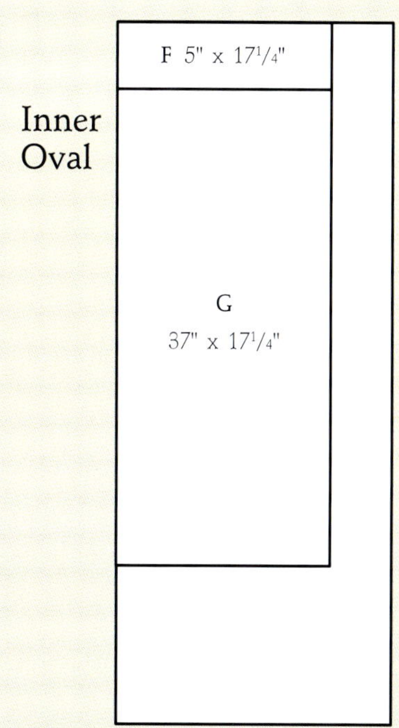

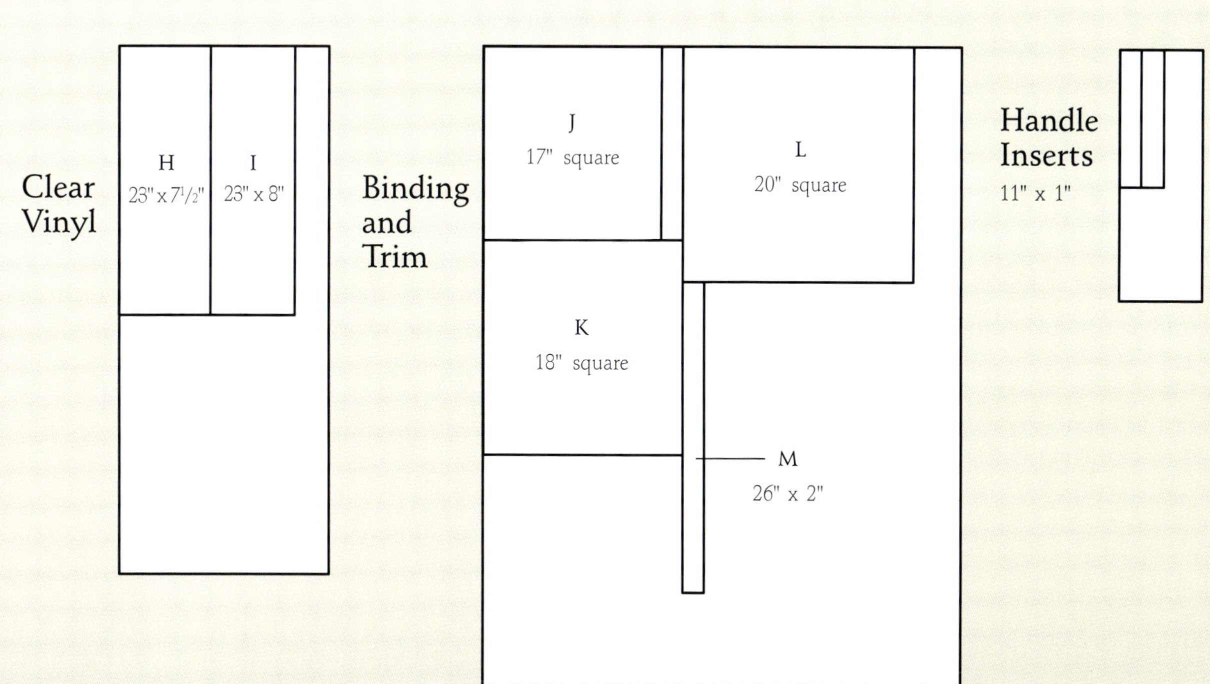

SOPHISTICATED GARMENT BAG
(shown on page 4)
pattern

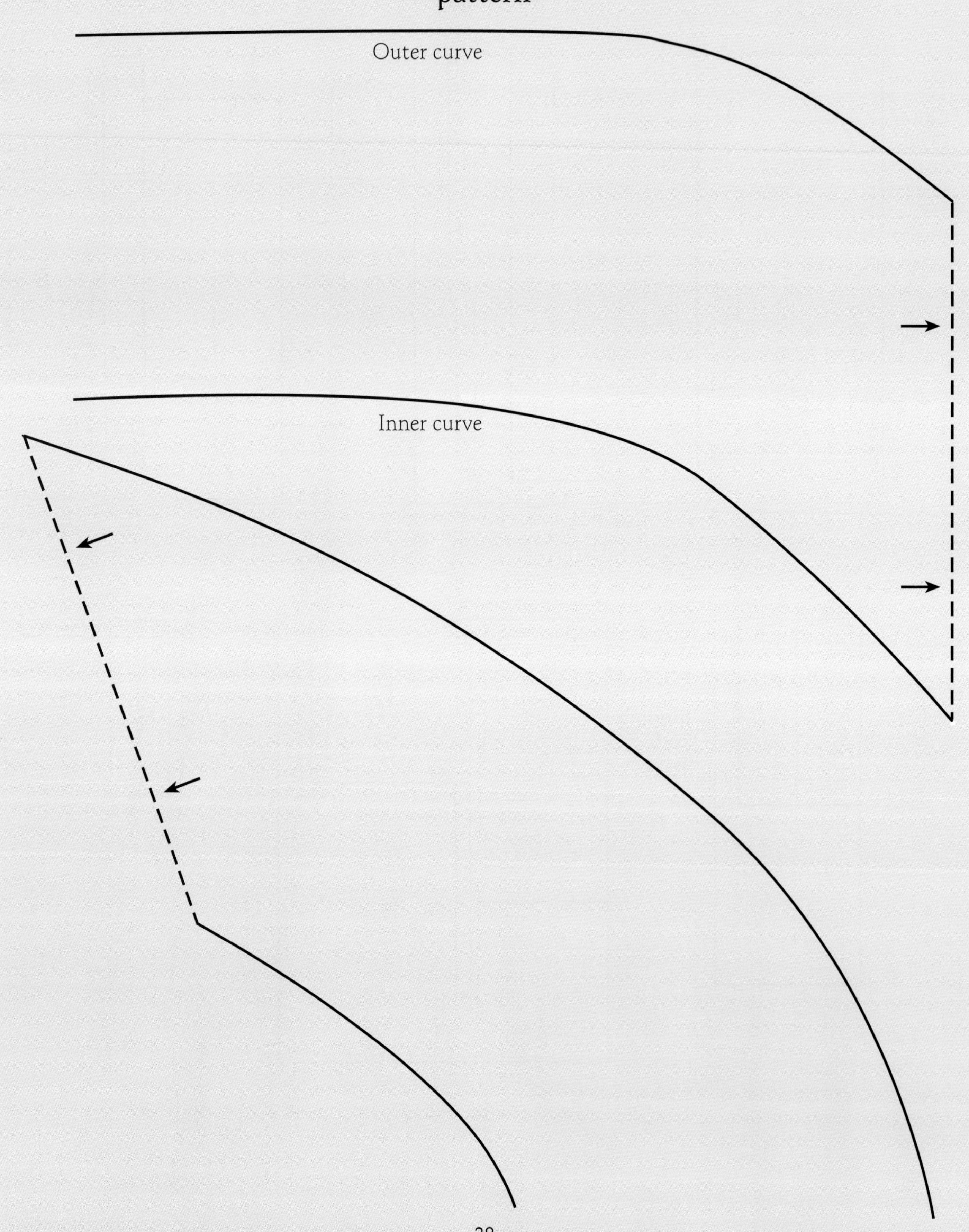

SOPHISTICATED CARRY-ALL
(shown on page 6)
cutting layouts

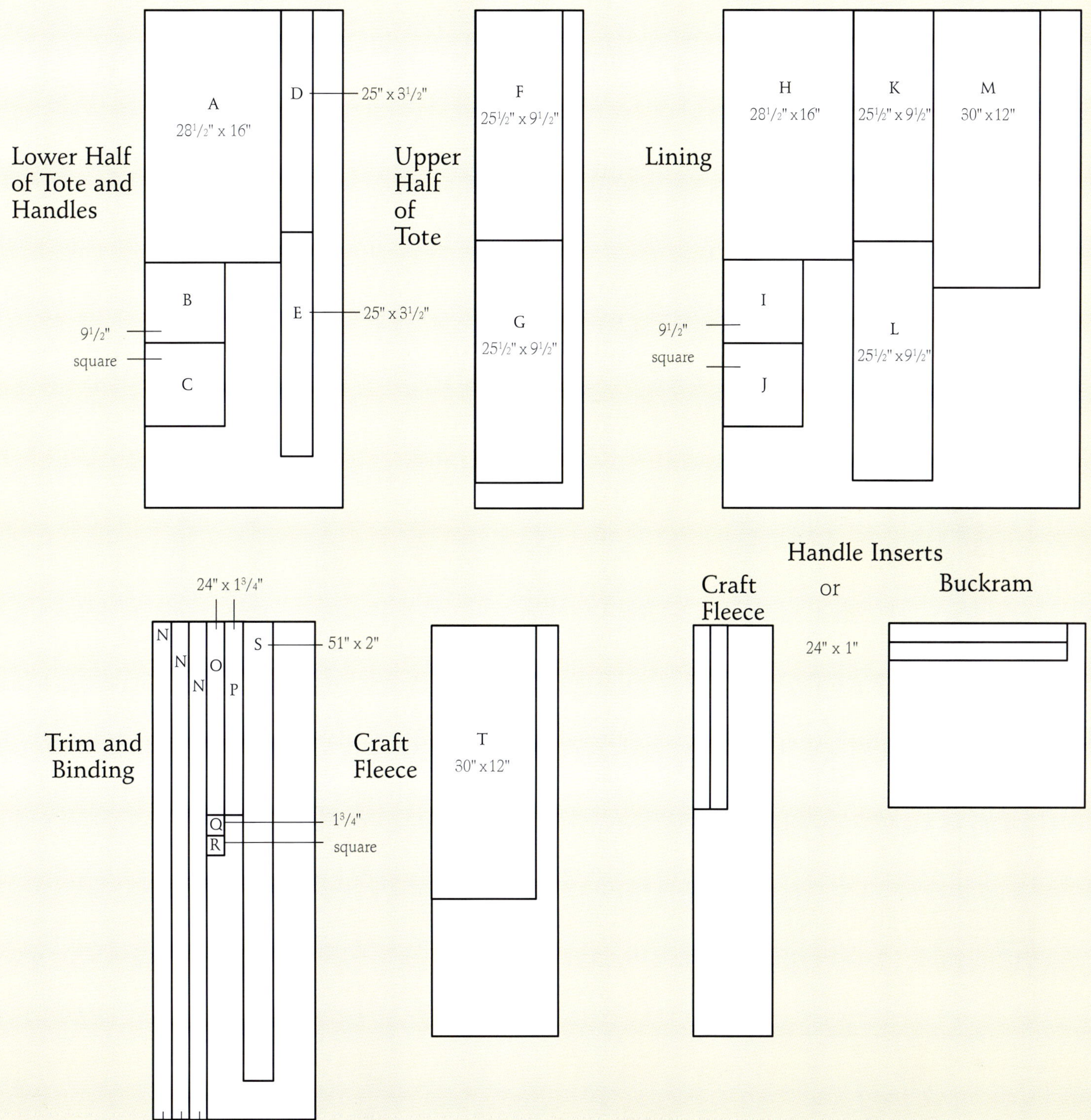

39

SOPHISTICATED COSMETIC BAG
(shown on page 8)
cutting layouts

Decorative Top

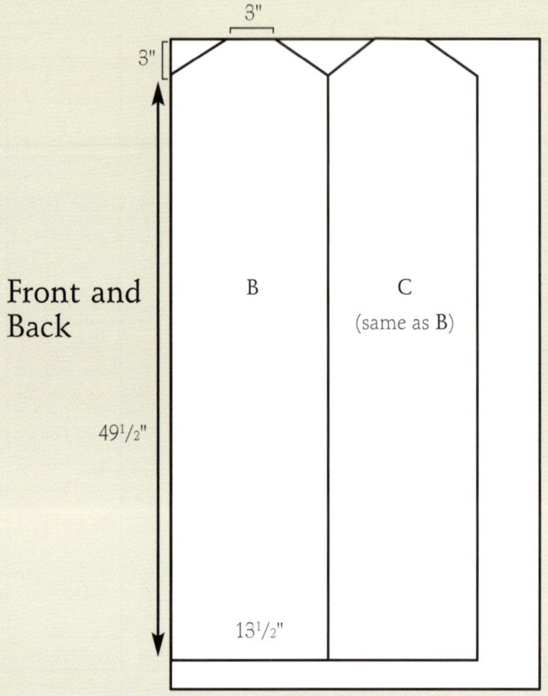

Front and Back

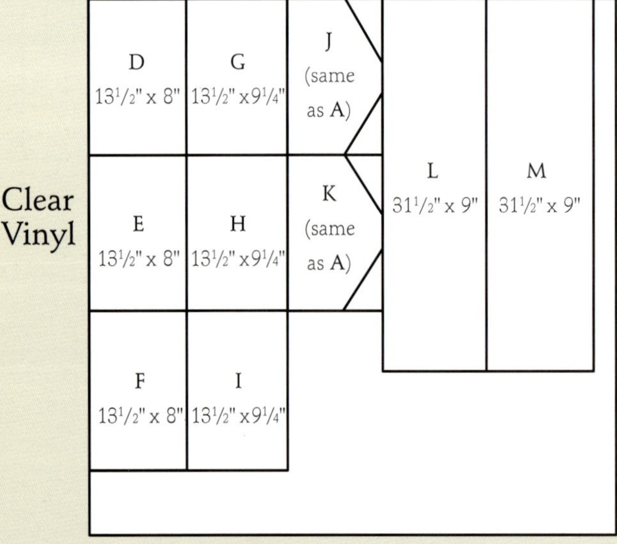

Clear Vinyl

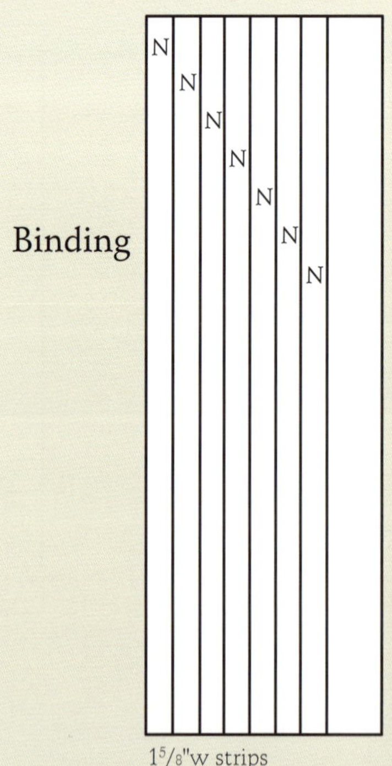

Binding

1 5/8"w strips

UNTAMED
(shown on page 14)
cutting layouts

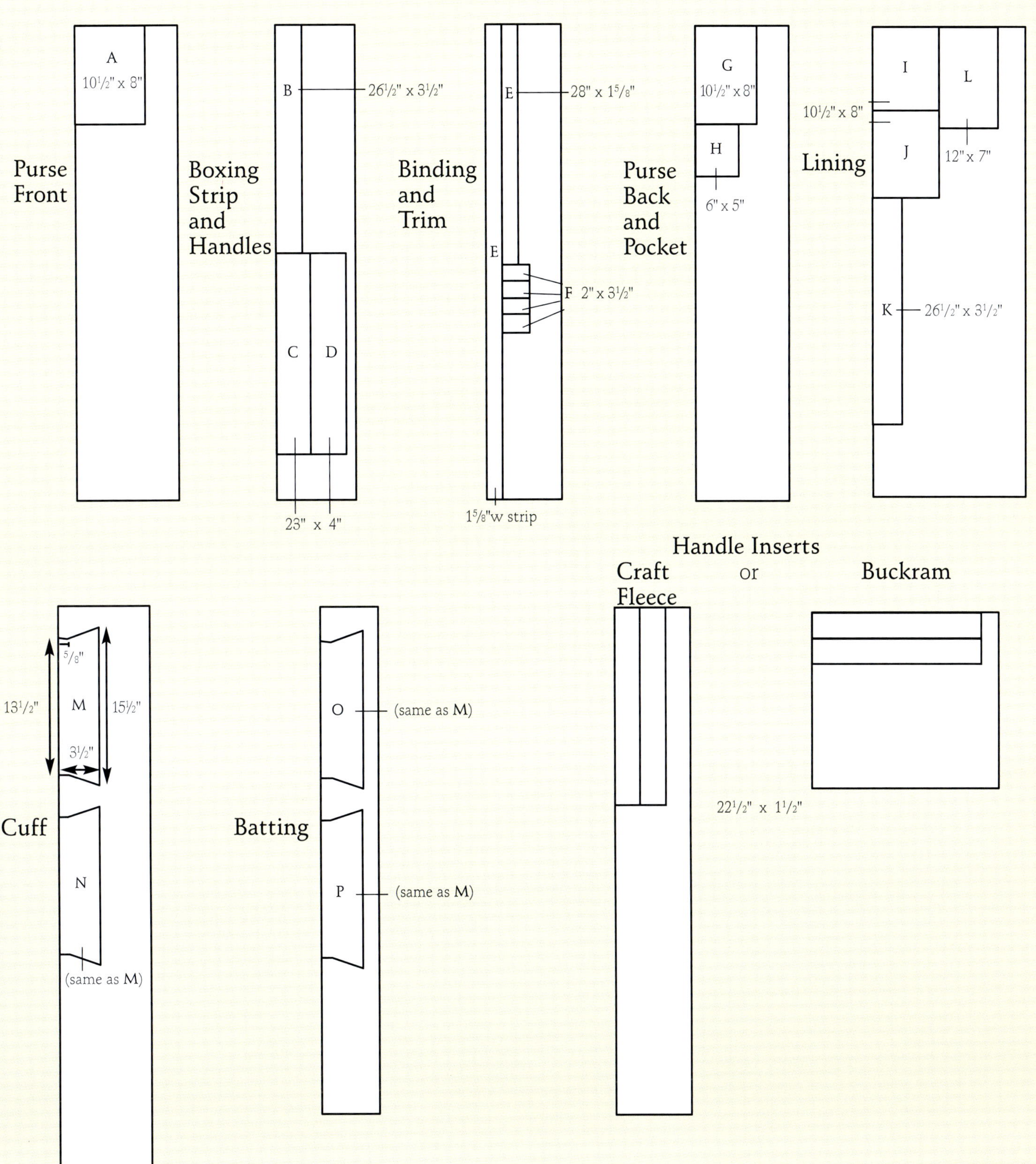

SLEEK
(shown on page 18)
cutting layouts

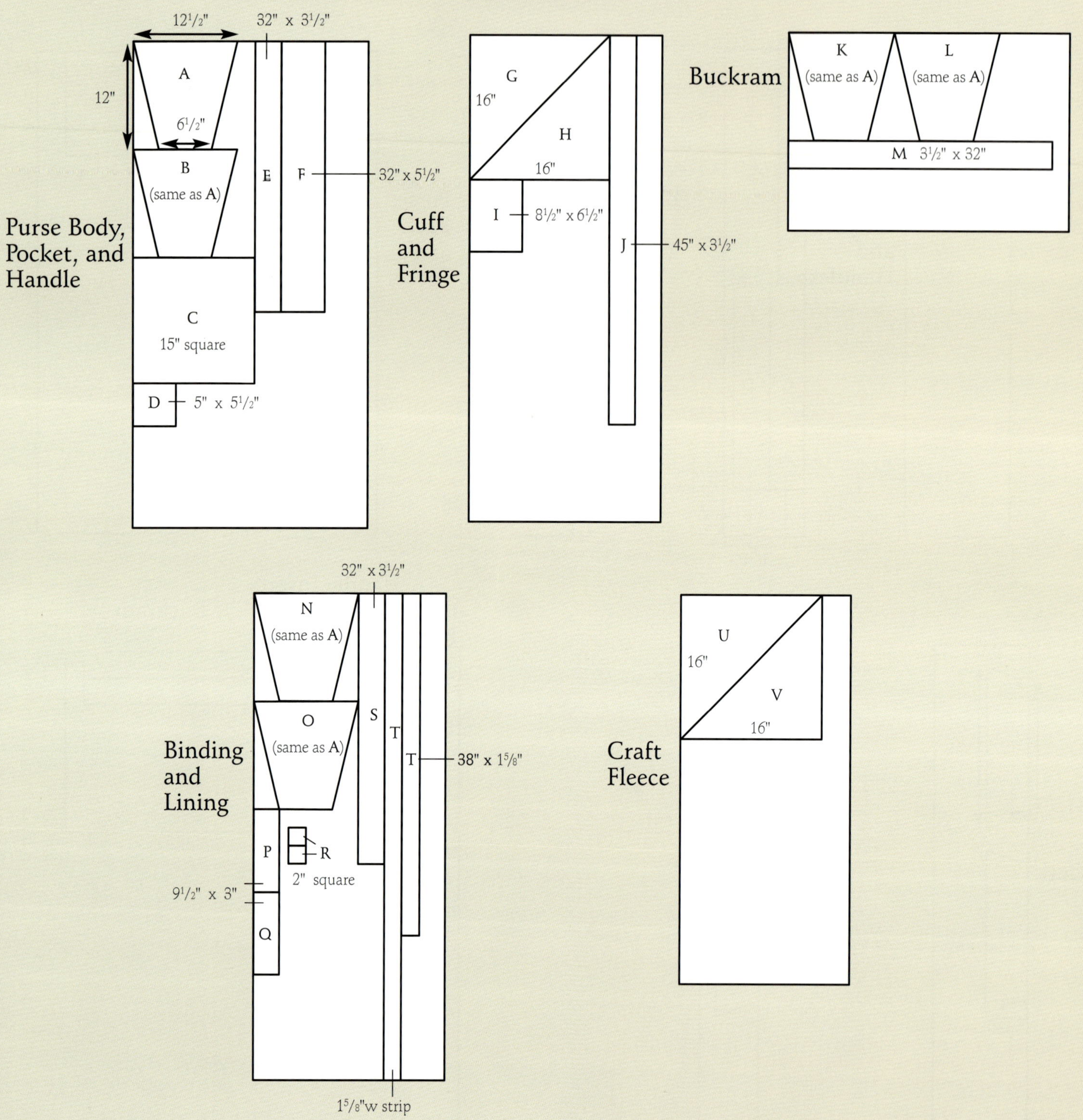

42

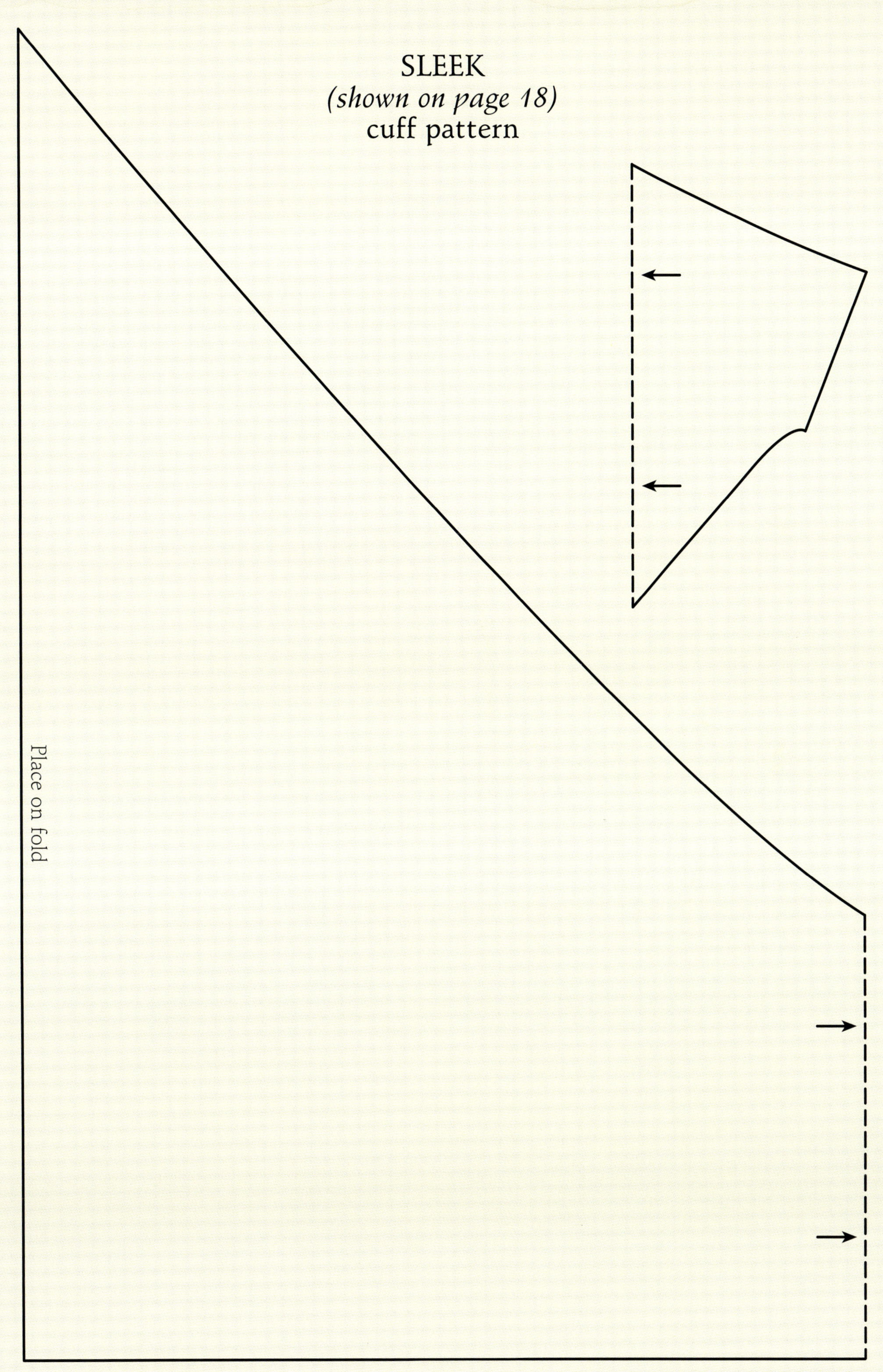

SLEEK
(shown on page 18)
cuff pattern
Place on fold

CHIC
(shown on page 22)
cutting layouts

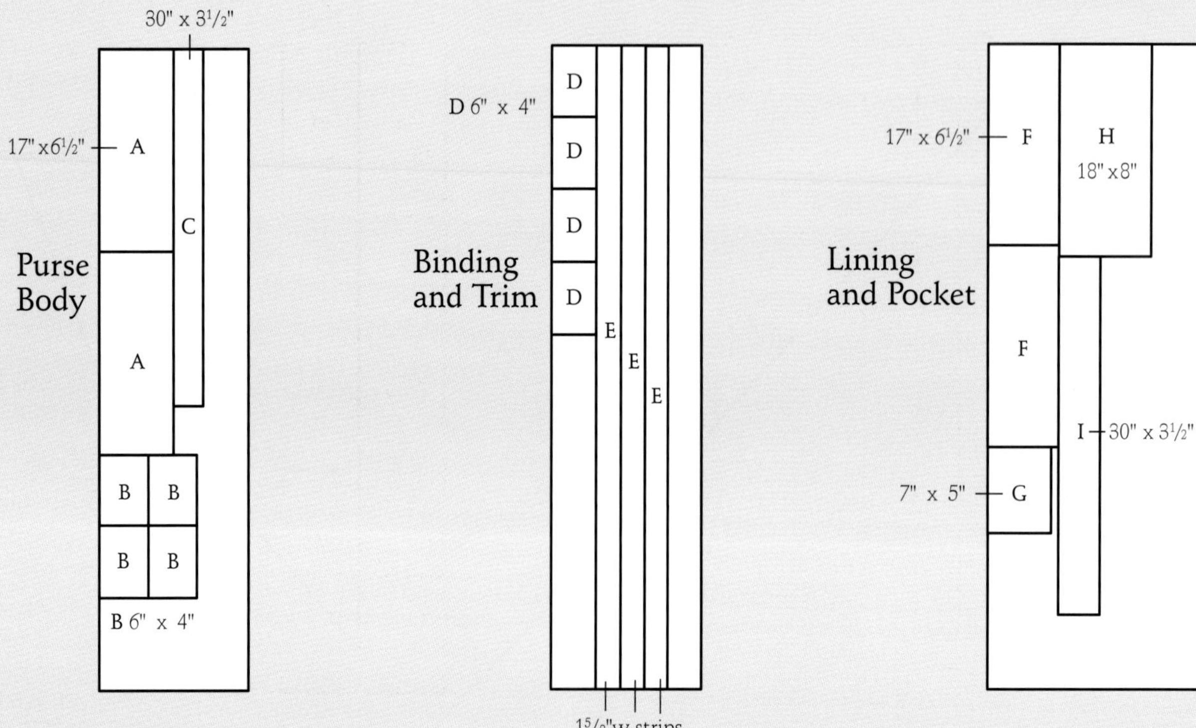

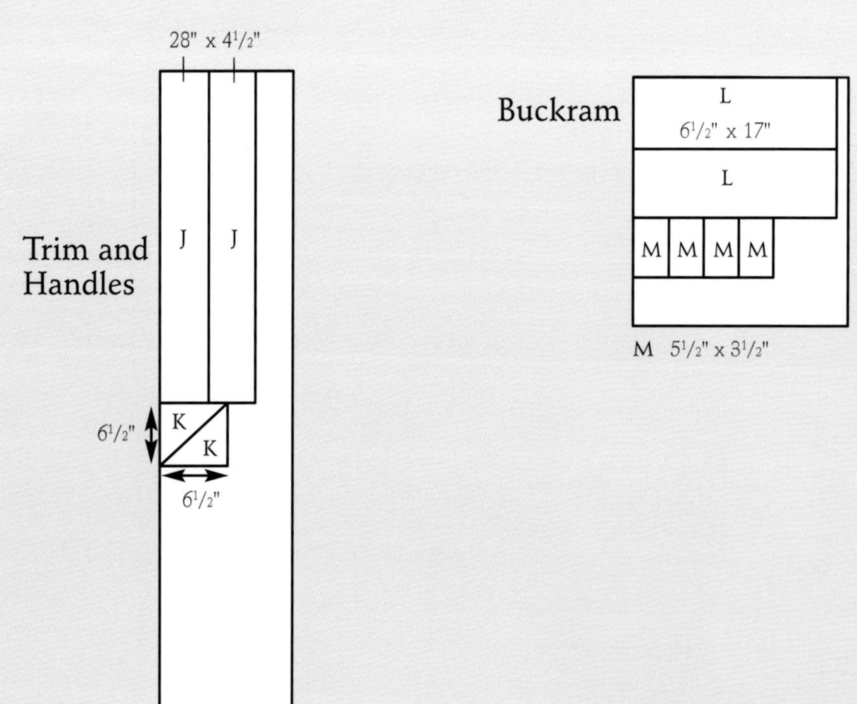

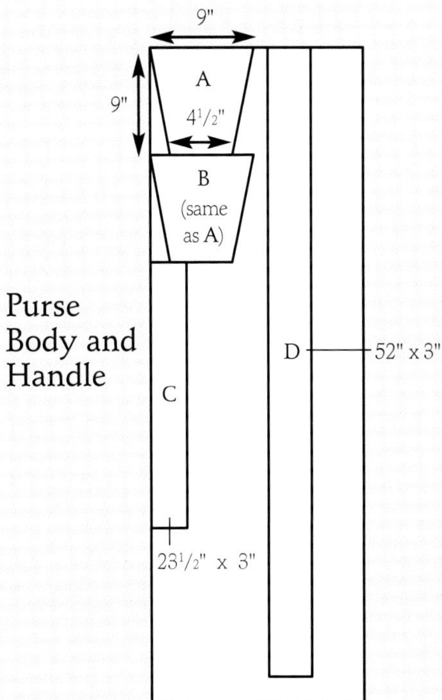

9"
A
9"
4¹/₂"
B
(same
as A)
Purse
Body and
Handle
D
52" x 3"
C
23¹/₂" x 3"

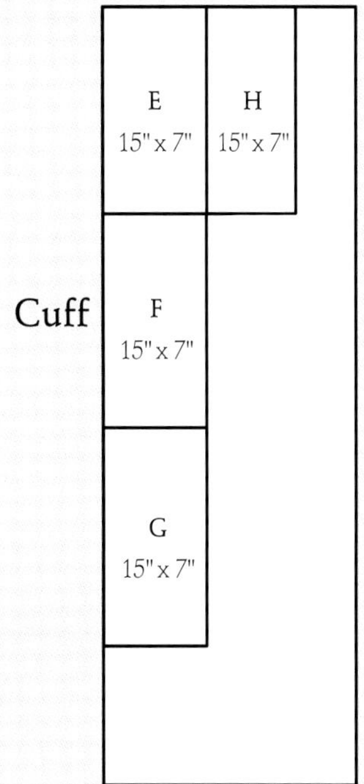

Cuff
E
15" x 7"
H
15" x 7"
F
15" x 7"
G
15" x 7"

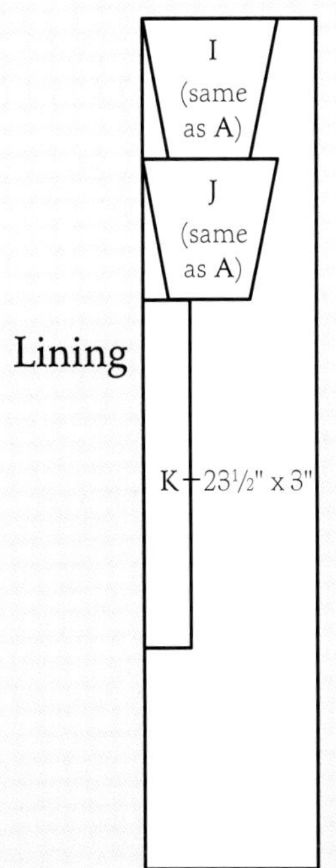

I
(same
as A)
J
(same
as A)
Lining
K
23¹/₂" x 3"

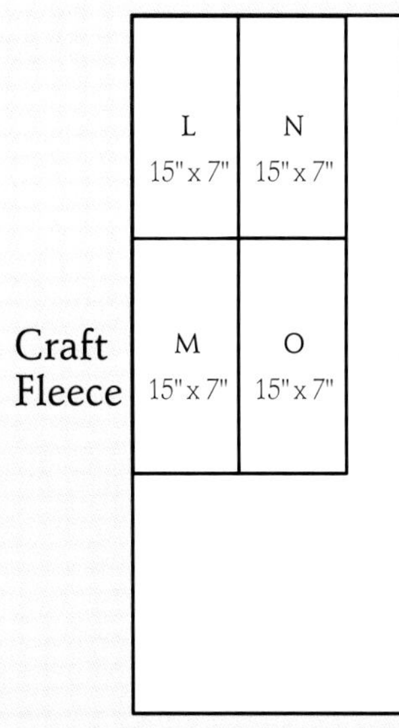

L
15" x 7"
N
15" x 7"
Craft
Fleece
M
15" x 7"
O
15" x 7"

THEATRICAL
(shown on page 26)
cuff pattern

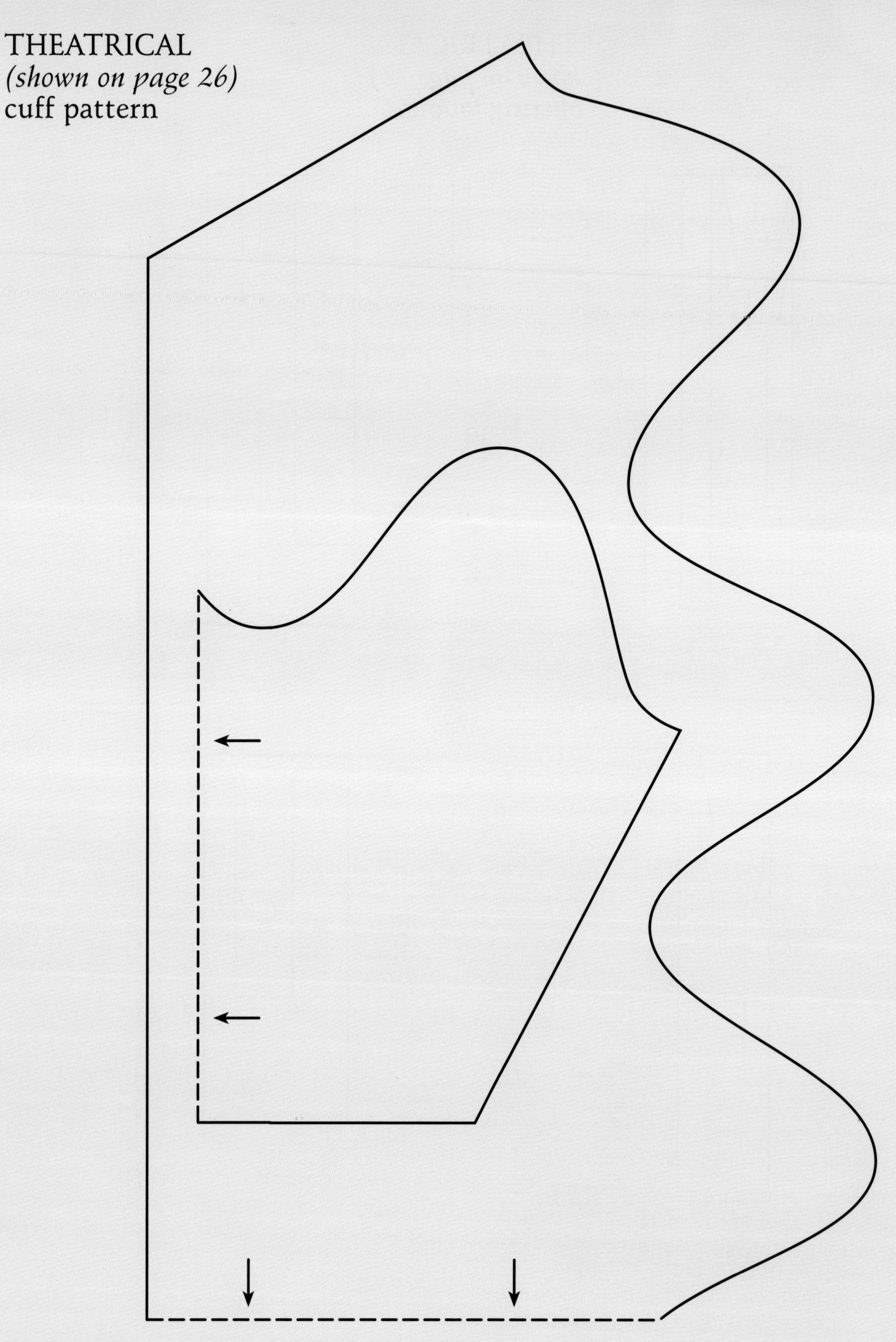

EXOTIC
(shown on page 30)
cutting layouts

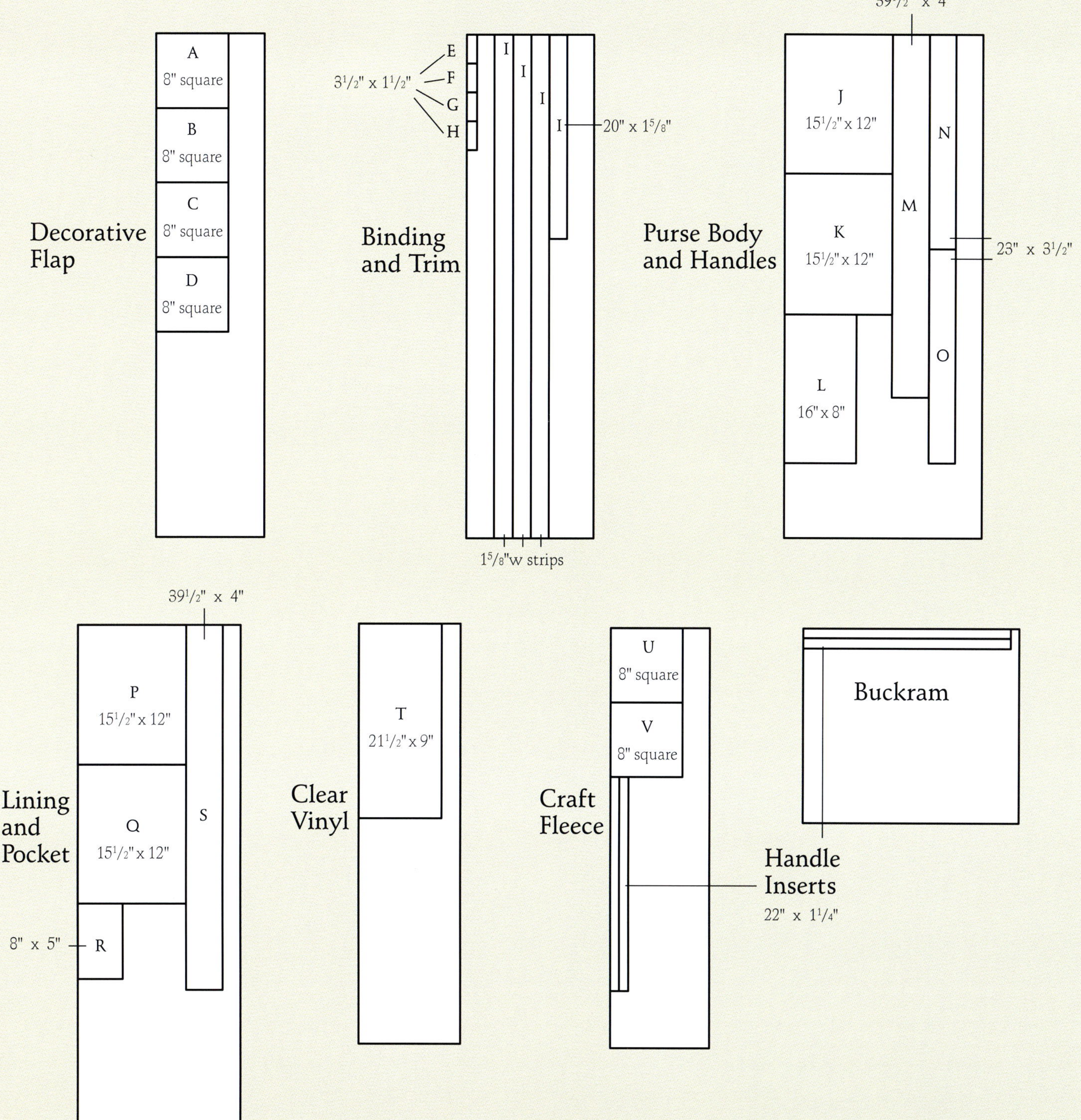

EXOTIC
(shown on page 30)
decorative flap pattern

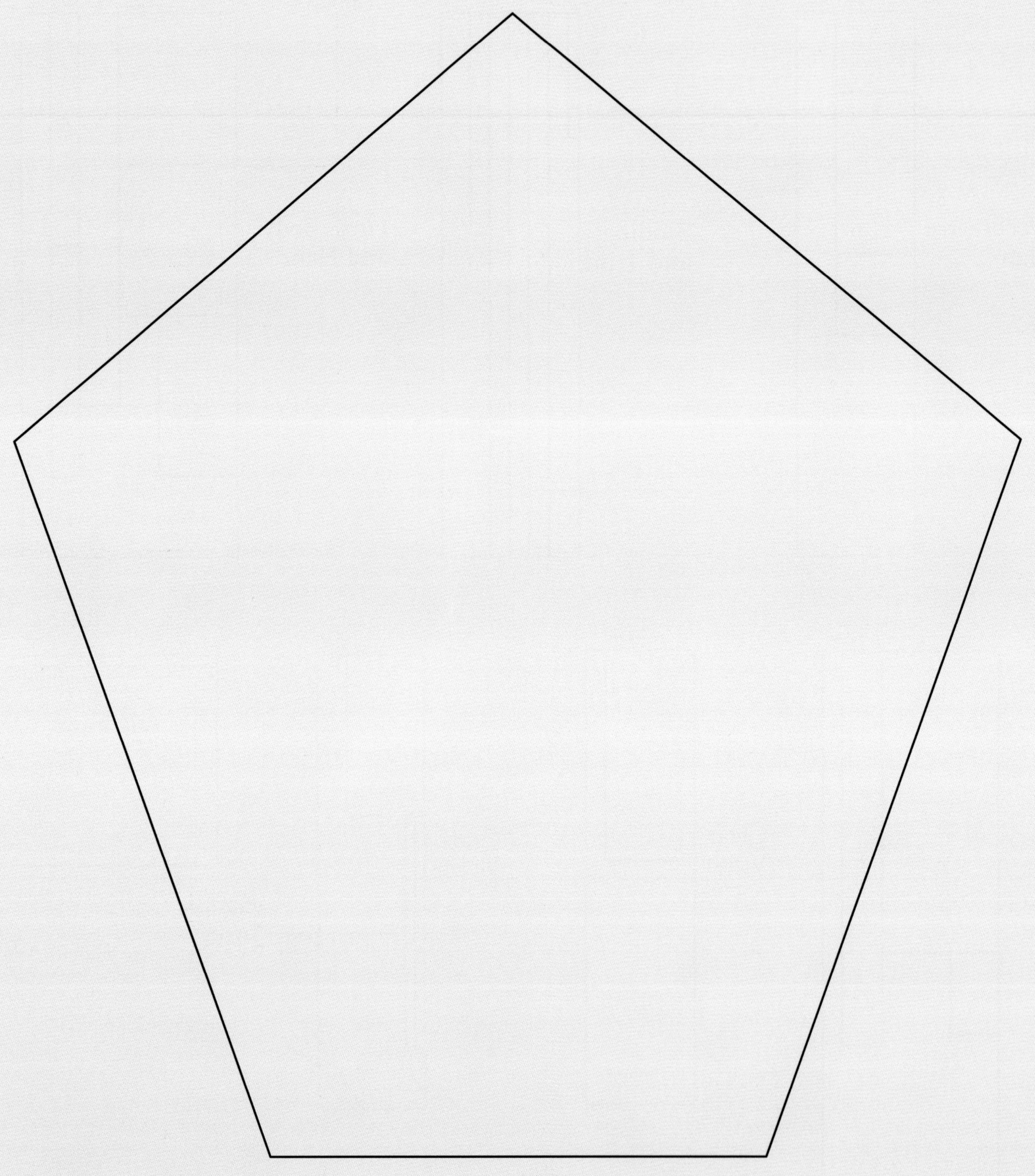

COSMOPOLITAN
(shown on page 34)
cutting layouts

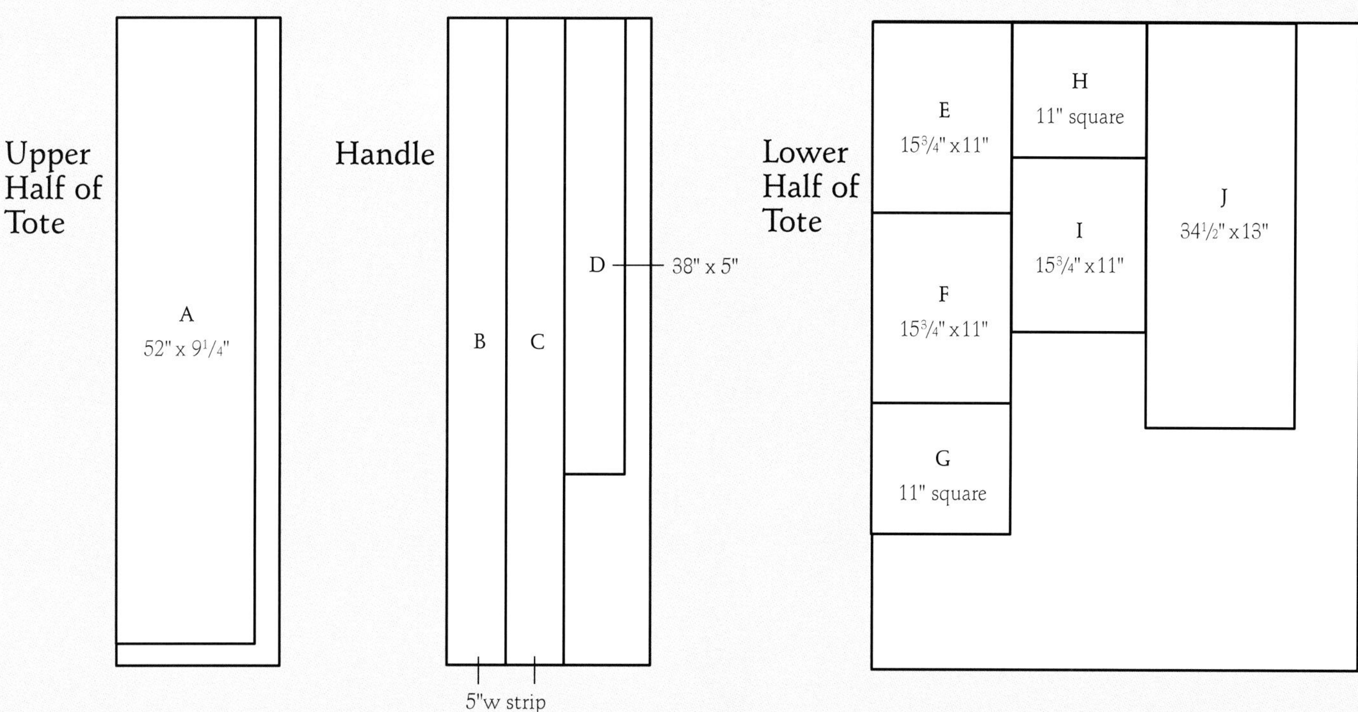

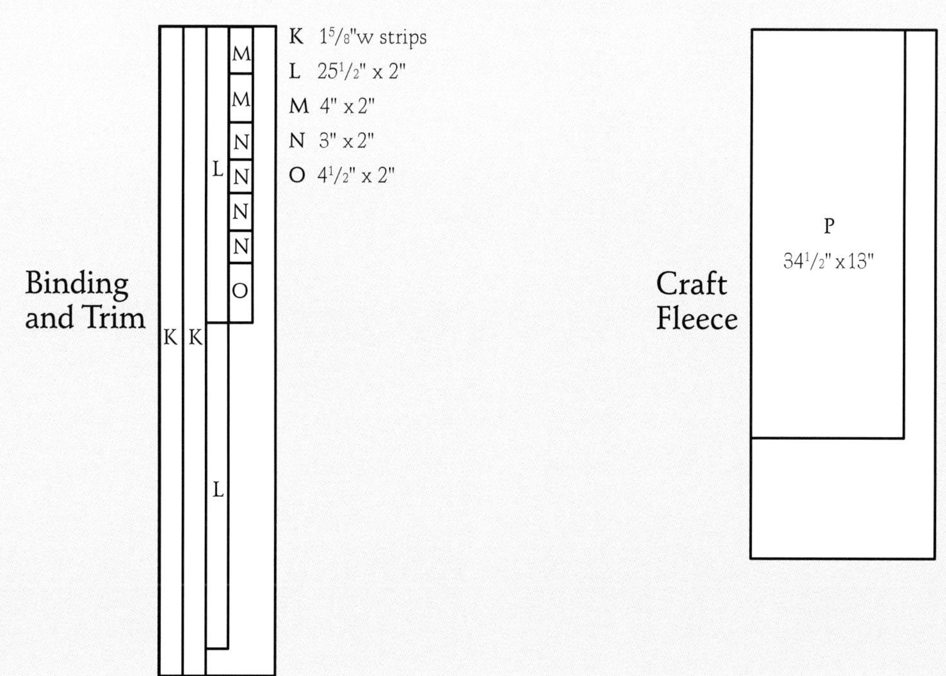

GENERAL INSTRUCTIONS

TOOLS

This list includes a few special tools you may want to use in making these projects. All items may be found in your favorite fabric store or on the Internet.

Bias tape maker – This gadget creates perfect bias tape or it may also be used for non-bias strips. Feed fabric through the wide end and press as it comes out folded on the small end. Our projects use $5/8$" and 1" bias tape makers.

Cutting mat – A cutting mat is a special self-healing mat designed to be used with a rotary cutter. A mat that measures approximately 18" x 24" is a good size for most cutting.

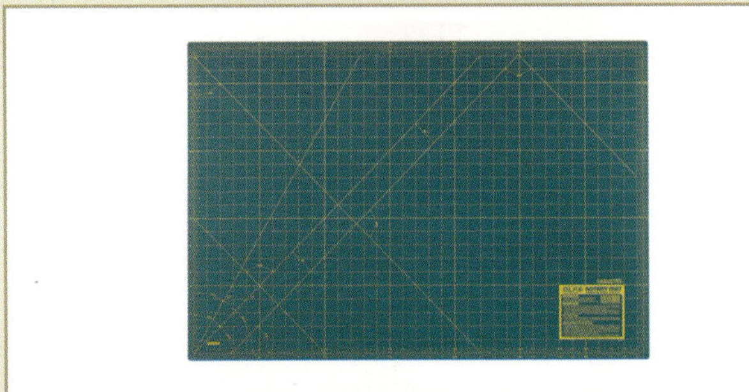

Ezy-Hem® Gauge – Use the measurements on the gauge for straight, even pressing.

Hem gauge – An alternative to the Ezy-Hem Gauge, the movable marker on this little ruler makes it easy to press folds accurately.

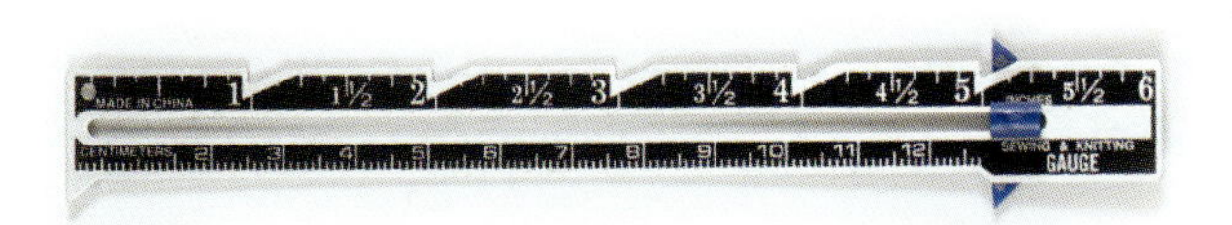

Jean-a-ma-jig™ – The Jean-a-ma-jig is a small piece of thick plastic that will help in sewing over bulky fabrics. To use, place your fabric under the presser foot; place the jean-a-ma-jig behind the fabric under the presser foot (see photo, page 54).

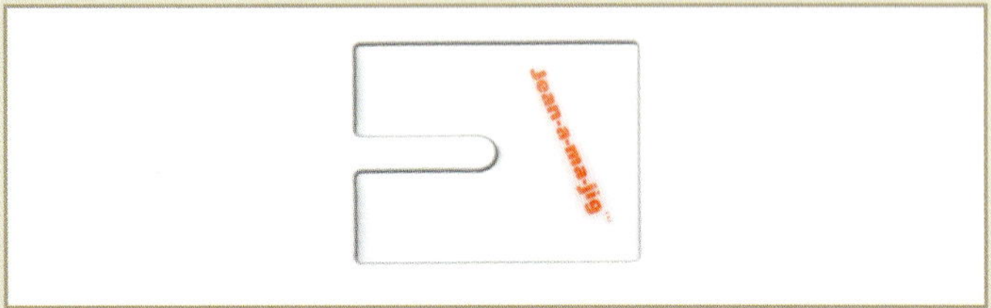

Needles – We recommend size 100/16 heavy-duty sewing machine needles for these projects as you will be stitching through several thick layers of fabric. Expect a few to bend or break.

Removable fabric marker – Look for a color that will show up well on your fabrics. Some markers disappear over time with exposure to air; some are removed with water. Test marker on a scrap piece of fabric to make sure the ink does not show on the right side.

Rotary cutter – The rotary cutter is an essential tool for quick, precise cutting. It should be used only with a cutting mat and rotary cutting ruler. Several sizes are available; we recommend the 45mm size. The rotary cutter blade is very sharp; for safety, immediately retract the blade or engage the blade guard after making each cut.

Rotary cutting ruler – A rotary cutting ruler is a thick acrylic ruler made specifically for use with a rotary cutter. It should have accurate $1/8$" crosswise and lengthwise markings. A 6" x 24" ruler is a good size for most cutting; a 15" square is helpful for cutting large pieces.

Sewing machine – You will need a sewing machine that produces an even straight stitch and zigzag stitch. Keep your machine clean and maintained.

SUPPLIES

The projects in this book require a variety of fabrics and notions. All items may be found in your favorite fabric store or on the Internet.

Buckram – Buckram is a loosely-woven stiff canvas used between fabric layers to add body. Look for it near the stabilizers in the fabric store.

Clear vinyl – Vinyls come in many thicknesses; choose one thin enough to sew through, but sturdy enough to wear well. To prevent clear vinyl from sticking to your sewing machine as you sew, pin tissue paper to it; gently tear tissue paper off when finished.

Decorator fabric – Choose sturdy fabrics that will wear well – your purse will be getting a lot of use! Choose tightly woven fabrics for binding to minimize fraying.

Magnetic snap kit – Magnetic snaps are easy to attach and use. Simply cut very small slits in the fabric and insert the brads of the snap. Place the flat plate over the brads on the other side of fabric and bend brads to hold snap in place.

Hem tape – We use hem tape for ease in sewing over clear vinyl. Any variety of hem tape in the suggested width can be used.

Rubberized fabric – This upholstery fabric has a coated backing so that it will not fray. Feel the back of the fabric – it will have a synthetic, rubbery feel.

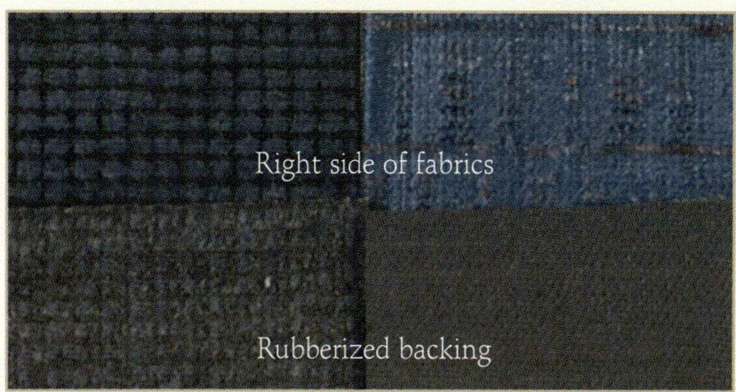

Zippers – Use nylon zippers with small teeth that can be sewn over and cut easily. If you can't find the length of zipper needed, look for "Make-A-Zipper." This zipper comes on a roll and can be cut to any length. The pulls are already attached. Zigzag stitch across the zipper to form the zipper stops, then use the zipper as you would any other.

CHOOSING FABRICS

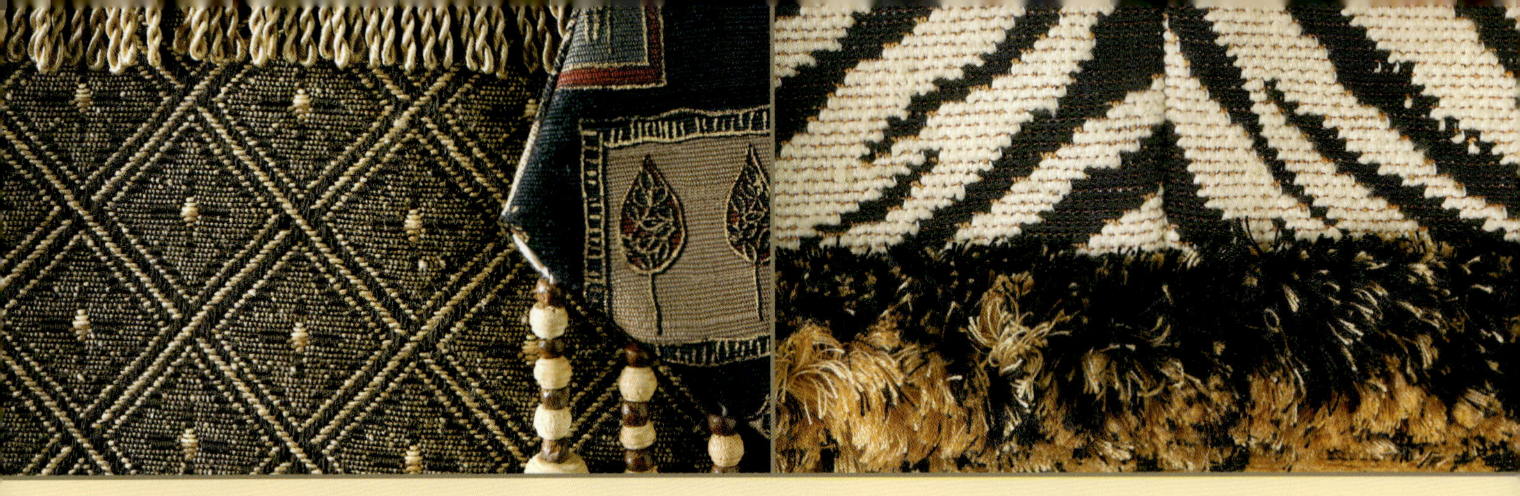

OUR PURSES FEATURE A VARIETY OF INTERESTING PRINTS AND BRIGHT COLORS, YET EVERYTHING WORKS TOGETHER. To get this look, choose a central element (a lush fringe, an eye-catching print) and add coordinating elements. For our Sophisticated travel pieces, page 3, we started with the fun diamond swirl print and added a solid black for binding and another black small print for accents. The monochromatic color scheme gives the effect of quiet refinement. On our Untamed purse, page 13, we chose a beautiful suede loop fringe and tiger print fabric as the base. The red stripe binding, the tan stripe cuff, and the green handles all pick up colors from the fringe. Don't be afraid to combine stripes and florals and even animal prints – the effect of the mix is stunning!

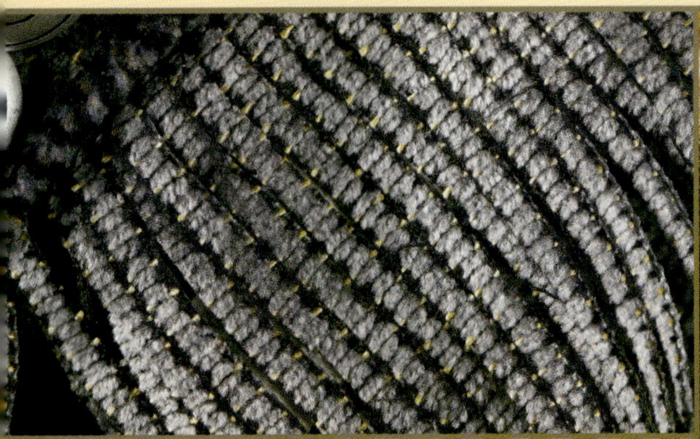

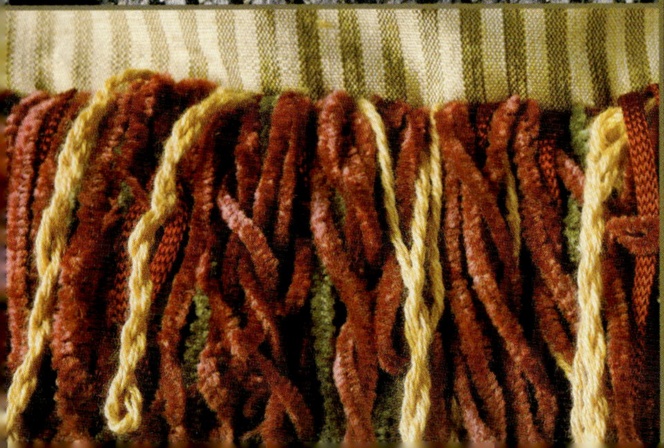

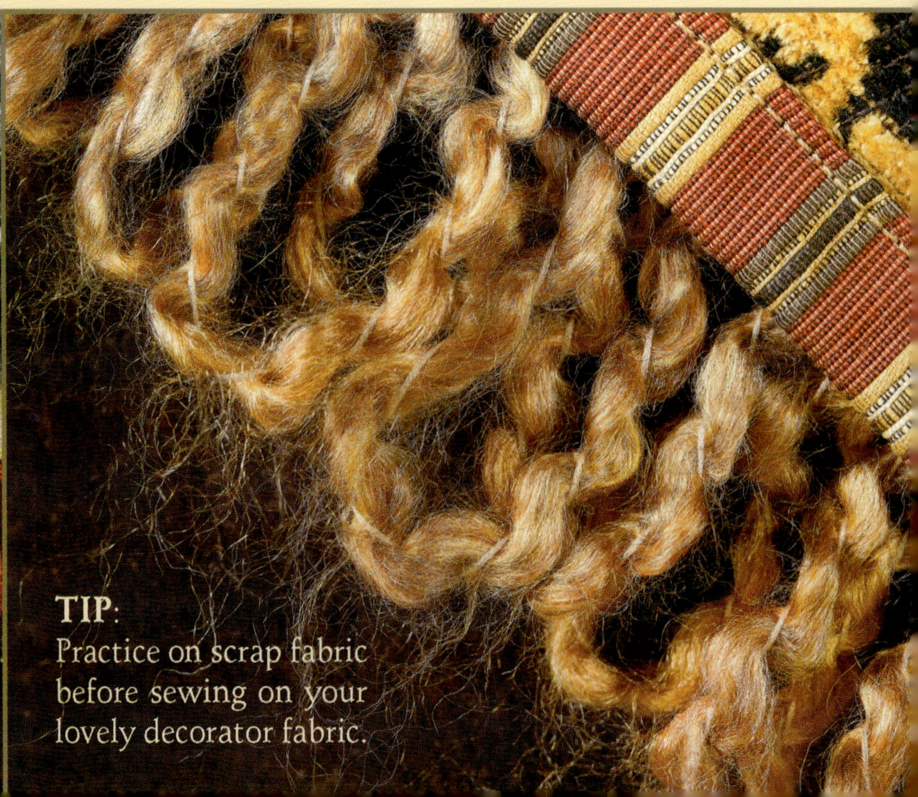

TIP:
Practice on scrap fabric before sewing on your lovely decorator fabric.

MAKING BIAS BINDING

1. Fold fabric square in half diagonally; cut on fold to make 2 triangles.

2. With right sides together and using a $1/4$" seam allowance, sew triangles together. Press seam allowances open.

3. On wrong side of fabric, draw lines the width specified in the project instructions. Cut off any remaining fabric less than this width. Mark seamlines $1/4$" from short edges of fabric.

4. With right sides inside, bring short edges together to form a tube.

5. Match raw edges so that first drawn line of section on top meets second drawn line of section on bottom. Insert pins through drawn lines at the point where drawn lines intersect, making sure the pins go through intersections on both sides.

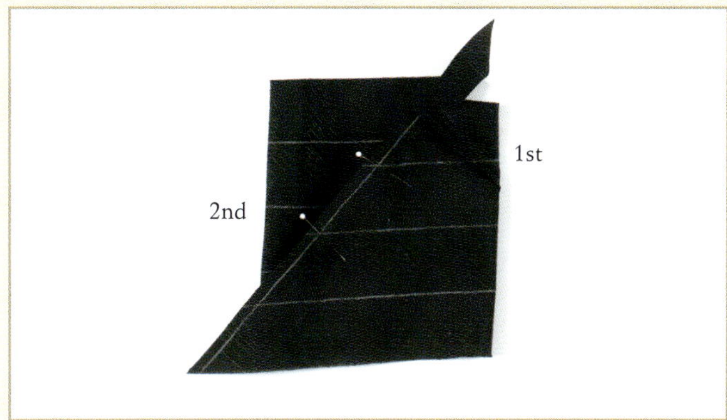

Using a $1/4$" seam allowance, sew edges together. Press seam allowances open.

6. To cut a continuous strip, begin cutting along first drawn line.

Continue cutting along drawn line around tube.

ATTACHING BINDING

Since the purse edges are bound, both sides of binding will show. We bound our edges so that the sides of the purse are the "wrong sides" of the binding and the purse front and back are the "right sides." Before attaching binding, pay close attention to which side of the seam should be the front, or right, side. Always sew binding to the wrong, or back, side of the seam first, then wrap it to the front and topstitch.

1. Press one long edge of binding $^1/_2$" to wrong side.

2. Matching right sides and raw edges and using a $^1/_4$" seam allowance, sew unpressed edge of binding to wrong side.

3. Wrap folded edge of binding around seam to front; pin and topstitch in place. If the seam is too thick, reduce the fold in the binding to $^1/_4$".

Front of finished binding

Back of finished binding

OVERLAPPING BINDING

When you bind the side seams of the purses, the binding will overlap with binding already sewn to the bottom seams of the purses.

1. Press short edges of binding $^1/_4$" to wrong side. Press one long edge $^1/_2$" to wrong side.

2. Carefully align one short pressed edge of binding with previously sewn binding; pin in place. Using a $^1/_4$" seam allowance, sew binding in place.

3. Wrap folded edge of binding around seam to front; pin in place. Use a Jean-a-ma-jig™ to guide the presser foot of your sewing machine as you begin sewing the binding. If the seam is too thick, reduce the fold in the binding to $^1/_4$".

MAKING AND ATTACHING HANDLES

Buckram inserts will make your handles stiff; craft fleece inserts will make your handles padded and soft. Follow cutting layouts to cut inserts from buckram or fleece, if desired.

1. For each handle, press short ends of fabric strip $1/2$" to wrong side; stitch in place.

2. Press each long side of fabric strip $1/2$" to wrong side. If your fabric will not hold a crease, you may need to use $1/2$"w fusible tape. Press each strip in half lengthwise, wrong sides together. Slide buckram or craft fleece, if desired, into handle, wrapping one $1/2$" fold around it. Topstitch $1/8$" from each long edge.

3. To attach handles, pin in place where desired. Place handle on bag at least as far onto bag as handle is wide.

4. Topstitch handle ends in place as shown.

SEWING BOX CORNERS

1. Aligning one short edge of boxing strip with top edge of purse front, pin boxing strip to purse front. At first corner, make a $1/8$" deep clip on boxing strip $1/4$" from corner. Pivot and stretch boxing strip to turn corner and continue matching raw edges and pinning. Repeat at remaining corner.

2. Sew boxing strip in place with a $1/4$" seam allowance. At each corner, shorten stitches to reinforce and stitch diagonally across corner instead of pivoting.

3. Repeat to sew boxing strip to purse back. Trim boxing strip that extends beyond purse front or back.

Metric Conversion Chart

Inches x 2.54 = centimeters (cm)	Yards x .9144 = meters (m)
Inches x 25.4 = millimeters (mm)	Yards x 91.44 = centimeters (cm)
Inches x .0254 = meters (m)	Centimeters x .3937 = inches (")
	Meters x 1.0936 = yards (yd)

Standard Equivalents

⅛"	3.2 mm	0.32 cm	⅛ yard	11.43 cm	0.11 m
¼"	6.35 mm	0.635 cm	¼ yard	22.86 cm	0.23 m
⅜"	9.5 mm	0.95 cm	⅜ yard	34.29 cm	0.34 m
½"	12.7 mm	1.27 cm	½ yard	45.72 cm	0.46 m
⅝"	15.9 mm	1.59 cm	⅝ yard	57.15 cm	0.57 m
¾"	19.1 mm	1.91 cm	¾ yard	68.58 cm	0.69 m
⅞"	22.2 mm	2.22 cm	⅞ yard	80 cm	0.8 m
1"	25.4 mm	2.54 cm	1 yard	91.44 cm	0.91 m

Production Team: Technical Writer – Michelle Mullman James; Technical Associate – Laura Siar Holyfield; Editorial Writer – Kimberly L. Ross; Photostylist – Cassie Newsome; Graphic Artist – Jenny Dickerson.